JERRY

SPRINGER

and laura morton

RINGMASTER!

BOXTREE

First published 1998 by St. Martin's Press, New York

This edition published 1999 by Boxtree
an imprint of Macmillan Publishers Ltd
25 Eccleston Place London SW1W 9NF
and Basingstoke

Associated companies throughout the world

ISBN: 0 7522 1345 8

9 8 7 6 5 4 3 2 1

A CIP catalogue record for this book is available from
the British Library.

Printed in Great Britain by The Bath Press, Bath

Given the fact that my parents, Richard and Margot Springer, dedicated their lives to Evelyn and me, the least I could do is dedicate this book to them.

Mom would have hated the show, Dad would have laughed at it, but they both let me know, every day we shared this life together, that there never was a moment that I wasn't loved.

My parents, Richard and Margot Springer, soon after they brought my sister, Evelyn, and me to America.

Contents

Acknowledgments

I would like to thank everyone from St. Martin's Press, including our publisher, Sally Richardson; our editor, Jennifer Weis; her assistant, Kristen Macnamara; Bob Wallace; art director, Steve Snider. Without their help, support, and guidance this book would not have been possible.

To my entire staff at *"The Jerry Springer Show"*: Without your incredible contributions, cooperation, and support, neither this project nor our show could ever have survived. Thanks to Richard Dominick, our executive producer, from whom all things flow regarding our show, I'm forever grateful.

And the rest of the team: Linda Shafran, who gives everything she has all the time; Carl Alaimo, Betsy Bergman, Lisa Bergman, Jennifer Byrne, Julianne Chelios, Melinda Chait, Rachelle Consiglio, Tracy Douglass, Ginger Damato, Mike Delazzer, Burt Dubrow, Lisa Farina, Laurie Fried, Alex Fronimos, Rhonda Funk, Bob Gassel, Annette Grundy, Christi Harber, Shara Hirsch, Gina Huerta, Steve Hyrniewicz, Dave Johnsen, Amy Jones, Greg Klazura, Nancy Kleinau, Brad Kuhlman, Tom Marvin, Mary Morelli, Terry Murphy, Ned Nalle, Mike O'Connor, Eric Olson :), Al Perales, Dan Puhar, and Kathy Posner (thanks so much for jumping in with both feet and helping us pull this together), Sheila Rosenbaum, Steve Rosenberg, Edi Schrammel, Todd Schultz, Jim Sherlock, Matt Sowder, Ryan Sucher, Chevette Weathersby, Steve Wilkos, Jennifer Williams, Jodi Yocom, Toby Yoshimura, Brenda You.

To Scott Barbour and everyone at Real Entertainment:

Thanks for everything. To my good friend and political inspiration, Mike Ford. To John Kiesewetter, you've always been a great resource. I really appreciate your support over the years. And thanks to Toria Tolley.

To my sister, Evelyn: At last, a family history in writing. I couldn't have done it without you.

To my agents, Mark Itkin, Jeff Kolodny, and Dan Strone: Somehow we managed to pull this one off. . . . Thanks for all of your determined dedication.

Micki Springer, Katie Springer: For living much of this book and my life.

To Jim Sperber: How can I ever thank you for all of the endless hours of research, interviews, photography selection, and too many other things on the list to mention? And last but not least, to Laura Morton, who was excited about this project even when I wasn't; who convinced me it was worth doing—and was right—who worked tirelessly at getting me to write about myself when I'd rather be reading about someone else. She made this happen: a total pleasure to work with, a class act, and a good friend.

ONE
In the Beginning

15 Minutes Before the Show

"Jerry, we're ready to brief you on today's guests."

"Okay. I'll be there in a minute. I'm almost done."

With a Punch in one hand (the cigar most appropriate for our show) and a pen in the other, I'm scribbling the last words down for the show's "Final Thought." What can I say about this one? It's too weird. A long puff, a quick glance out my window at Lake Michigan, and it suddenly comes to me, so I reduce it to paper. Then it's "Take care of yourself and each other." A sip of Starbucks' Caffe Mocha, I grab a tie, hand my commentary to Brian, who'll put it on the TelePrompTer, and then a few strides down to Richard Dominick's office for the two-minute briefing that takes place before every show.

The executive producer's office resembles a miniature music hall of fame. Pictures of Frank Sinatra and Elvis Presley line the wall behind the desk. Baseball has its place as well. He's especially proud of his Keith Hernandez baseball card collection. Richard's office is the center of the universe for *"The Jerry Springer Show."* I miss the pool table that used to be where the conference table is now. At least he kept his pinball machine.

The briefing begins. The show producer explains: "Today we have a story about a man who cut off his own penis. He was apparently being stalked by another man and thought this was the only way this other guy would lose interest. He used garden shears to cut it off."

So I'm thinking: *If he wanted to lose this guy, why didn't he just change his number?*

Richard, ever the executive producer, is asking whether or not the producer has actually verified the story. She has and shows us all the pictures. Richard's sitting behind his desk, as usual, conducting the meeting as if he were conducting the New York Philharmonic, using his stogie as his conductor's wand. He's smooth, calm, but direct.

Behind his desk, I glance at the ceramic Elvis lamp. I smile, thinking about "the King," and do an impromptu hip wiggle I know he'd be proud of. I grab a baseball bat and take a few swings as I listen to the rest of the briefing. Behind me is a large board that lays out the schedule of shows for the next three months. As the producer finishes her orientation, I take one final swing of the bat and say, "Let's make this our greatest show ever."

Everyone heads out and makes their way to the set.

7 Minutes Before the Show

I'm off to hair and makeup. Linda Shafran, head of publicity, stops me en route to introduce me to two visitors from one of our affiliates. I walk down the bright white hallway tiled with faux marble linoleum. The sound of my shoes is amplified by the echo in the corridor. I can hear the audience in the faint background as Todd Schultz, our stage manager, gives them the guidelines for the show.

4 Minutes Before the Show

"Can you believe today's topic?" Ginger, my makeup artist, asks as she applies her final touch.

I glance in the mirror, patting down a flyaway curl, wondering with a face like this how'd I ever get into television? She delints my dark suit as I slip my jacket on. Armani can mask countless flaws.

2 Minutes Before the Show

Standing backstage I realize I have tickets for the Chicago Bulls game tonight that I can't use. I'll give them to Todd. The audience sounds full of energy. This ought to be a good show. I clear my throat one last time before I make my way onstage to do my opening shtick.

1 Minute Before the Show

"I just got a new cable contract . . . " (The audience cheers at this news.)

"Yeah, they're coming next Thursday to install it." (The audience groans—as usual.)

"I was in LA last week, filming my movie. This gorgeous woman is pounding on my hotel room door for two hours." (The audience goes wild chanting, "Jer-ry! Jer-ry! Jer-ry!")

"So finally I let her out. . . . " (The audience laughs, as I continue to tell them the same jokes I have told every audience for seven seasons.)

I finish my impersonation of a struggling Catskill comedian and make a dash backstage. . . . I think to myself: "It's show time!"

1st Minute of the Show

"Hi, and welcome to the show. You know, over the past six years I've interviewed many unusual people with unbelievable stories . . . but what you're going to hear today is absolutely astonishing. Today, in an exclusive interview, we're going to talk to Earl, a man who cut off his own penis . . .

"He did it with a pair of gardening shears identical to these . . .

"Okay, Earl is here to tell us his story for the very first time. But before we meet Earl, take a look at some news footage from his hometown."

(The news footage begins on the monitors in the studio.)

Amidst earlier reports that someone broke into the victim's apartment, Earl has now confessed to cutting off his own penis and is reportedly in fair condition at the hospital tonight. Earl admitted to police that he used an ultrasharp gardening tool to dismember himself and later flushed the remains down the toilet . . .

Oh, my God—I'm feeling sick. I'd rather *die* than cut off my own manhood. Okay—maybe not die—at least not yet.

Well, I don't know that I'd want to die just yet. I mean, if I did, can you imagine my obituary?

JERRY SPRINGER IS DEAD!

OBITUARY

Jerry Springer, the man critics refer to as the "king of sleaze," died early this afternoon while taping his show "I Cut Off My Manhood!" Efforts to revive him failed as a transsexual and a stripper, fighting over who would give him mouth-to-mouth resuscitation, were clobbered by a mother of the Klan wielding what looked like a burning cross from a now broken chair. Springer, the Ringmaster of the three-ring circus known as *"The Jerry Springer Show,"* went out on top with his show rated number one in the country. No one knows exactly why anyone watched it . . . though most speculate that the outrageousness of his guests was simply an outlet and escape for his viewers. Springer's death comes none too soon for those who saw him as the godfather of Western civilization's demise.

Mr. Springer, a graduate of Northwestern University School of Law, the former mayor of Cincinnati, and ten-time Emmy-winning news anchor and commentator, was 54.

That seems like a reasonable description, but how would my own city cover my death?

WMAQ, Chicago

"Our lead story tonight: Beloved talk show host Jerry Springer died today while taping his show. The details of his demise are unclear. This television legend set new standards in broadcasting, constantly offering us thought-provoking, entertaining, and often compelling issues throughout the seven years of *"The Jerry Springer Show."* It is believed that the topic being discussed during the taping earlier today was "I Cut Off My Manhood!" Of course he was a favorite here in Chicago, and of this station. We will all miss him very much. Carol Marin will be here later for a special report."

Yeah, right!

New York Post headline

SPRINGER KICKS (THE BUCKET)

or

SPRINGER GOES DOWN FIGHTING!

(Of course, with the accompanying photo of Jerry falling through the audience.)

Outside the NBC Tower in Chicago, a large group of "Springer Heads" has gathered to pay their final respects to the man they referred to as "Jer-ry, Jer-ry, Jer-ry!" The song "Kung Fu Fighting" could be heard solemnly playing in the background.

And what if I really did die? Would I go to Heaven or Hell? Would anyone care? Like everything in my life, I'd probably be taken to task for being the "Ringmaster" of the circus that has been the life and times of Jerry Springer. Sometimes I think there's no way I'd ever get past those pearly gates—but hypothetically, *what* if I did?

"Hey! What's going on? Where am I? I don't know what's happening."

(Suddenly the door swings open and the producer says)

"Okay, Jerry, you're on in five minutes. You've got to be really energetic and upbeat. Try not to smile too much because it'll make you seem insincere. You remember everything we talked about, right? Are you ready, big guy? Let me take a look at you. Man, you seem nervous. Are you all right?"

"No, I'm not all right! Where the hell am I? And who are you?"

"I'm Morty, the producer you spoke to about being on the show."

"Morty? Producer? What are you talking about? Where am I?"

"Jerry, you can't do this to me. You promised you'd go on. This is my ass if you bail on me now! You of all people should know how it is right before a taping. Help me out here. Say you'll go through with it."

"Go through with what? Where am I?"

"It's God's talk show, man! You're our lead guest. You gotta get out there or I'm a dead man. Okay, I'm already dead. But you know what I mean."

"Talk show! I'm not doing any talk show. I don't care *who* the host is. I made a vow that I'd never be a guest on a talk show, and I'm sure as hell not going to start now."

"Hey, we don't use the *H* word up here. You don't get it, do you? You don't have a choice. This isn't about talk . . . it's about defending your life, which, considering your life, perhaps you ought to hang loose till Johnny Cochran passes this way."

"Defend my life? Are you trying to tell me that . . . I'm dead?"

"Well, you're sitting in Heaven's green room getting ready to go on God's talk show. What do you think?"

Jeezel, what happened? One minute I'm hosting my own talk show, the next I'm appearing on God's. And what's this about having to defend my life? Sure, I've had a few, okay, maybe more than a few mistakes to account for, but I've always stepped up to the plate and taken responsibility. And now this! I'm supposed to appear in front of God himself and try and explain this craziness that's been my life? Where would I begin? It's not like I can leave anything out. He'll know I'm not telling the whole truth. But if I do tell it all, he'll send me to Hell.

(Suddenly, there's a knock at the door.)

"Hi, Jerry, we decided to push your segment back, so you've got a few extra minutes before you're on. Why don't you have a seat and relax? I'll be back to get you."

"Who are you?"

"I'm Reverend Flager, Morty's associate producer. Did you need anything else?"

Oh, damn!

(I'm pacing the room as I flip on the television in the green room. I hear . . .) " . . . that's right, you can order the 'Too Hot for Heaven' videos if you call now. They're the best uncensored moments from the number-one show of all time."

Well, that sounds familiar.

"Live from Cloud 9. It's God's Talk Show! Tonight, join God and his guests, Mother Teresa and Jerry Springer. With Elvis Presley and the Heavenly Orchestra . . . and now, please welcome the real 'King' of all mediums . . . GOD!"

(The crowd goes crazy as they chant, "Yah-Weh! Yah-Weh! Yah-Weh!")

"Hi, and welcome to the show. I'm GOD, your host, and boy, do we have a great show for you tonight!

First, we've got Mother Teresa, who just arrived from her latest mission. She's going to tell all about her good-will trip. And we have Jerry Springer, who just arrived via Chicago. I'm uncertain as to what to do with Springer, and I'd like you to help me decide his fate. Will he stay here with us in Heaven, or should we send him straight to—well, you know where—or do we give him a little more time back on earth to try and improve himself? Who knows how this'll turn out? So keep your dial and your faith set right where it is. We've got a lot of surprises in store for you—and for Jerry—so let's get going. . . ."

What is he talking about?

" . . . and now, put your wings together and please give a heavenly welcome to Jerry Springer. . . . "

Oh, God, how am I ever going to get through this? Should I wave to the crowd? Do I shake God's hand? What if he doesn't like me?

"Hi, Jerry, and welcome to the show."

"Glad to be here . . . I think. . . . "*(So far, so good . . .)*

"Well, well, well, you've been a busy guy. Tell us what you've been up to."

"Until recently, I *thought* I was having the time of my life.

Now I'm not so sure. Maybe you can help shed some light on the subject."

"Come now, Jerry, surely you've figured out that shedding light on your life is exactly what we're here for. Tell us about your recent projects. I hear you were writing a book?"

"Uh, well, yes, I *was* writing a book. I'm calling it *RING-MASTER!* which seems to be a fitting description for my life, particularly in recent years. It's been pretty much of a circus. Even in the beginning—my life was never dull."

"Why don't you give the folks a little background about yourself."

"Okay, good idea." *(I'll go for a little drama here, although it's all true.)*

Me—the last time I was cute.

11

"I was born in the midst of a bombing campaign over London . . . Hitler's last effort at reversing his imminent and far-too-long-in-coming demise. Late during the evening of February 13, 1944, I came, according to Mom, loudly and boisterously, wailing into the world . . . the second child of Richard and Margot Springer . . . and, as a whole lot of observers to my life can attest, I haven't closed my mouth since.

"And yet there really is nothing in that now distant past, or in the years of my childhood that followed, that gave one any clue as to what I would ultimately become—the Ringmaster of the most outrageous show on television—depending on your point of view, either its craziest, most compelling hour . . . or its worst."

"But, Jerry, surely you'd agree that there was always a little bit of 'show biz' in you—you were always playing a role of some kind, even as a young child."

"Oh, God, yes!—Uh . . . can I call you God?"

"Sure, everyone does."

"Well, even as a young child living in London I would act out all sorts of roles. From the fourth-floor flat my family lived in I would watch as the double-decker buses would make their circular turns right outside our window, pretending I was the bus driver. I took one of my mother's trays from the kitchen and used it as the steering wheel. That was such a thrill for me to actually *be* the bus driver. When I came to America, my cousin Sid took me to the local firehouse, and then all I wanted to be was a fireman. Or I'd listen to the radio and want to be a DJ, spinning the same four 78s we had on our old Victrola—Patti Page, Frankie Lane, Bing Crosby, Frank Sinatra.

"Oh, you'll appreciate this story, God. I'd come back from synagogue after high holy day services and spend the next few days standing on my desk with a blanket wrapped around my shoulders, chanting gibberish, pretending it was Hebrew. I was determined to be a rabbi. The point being, if something seemed interesting to me, I'd want to be it . . . my joy was always defined by *being* something. In fact, it didn't even have to be real. In Miss Eisenson's fifth-grade class, I wore a Superman outfit under my clothing. Thankfully, there was no phone booth around. Jumping out of the second-floor window could've been real painful.

"In any event, I always remember being happy. My active and fertile imagination played no small part in that. It's remained the same throughout my adult life. Hey, it'd be great being a mayor. Wow, how about a news anchor. I think I'd like to make a record, sing on a tour, write a book. Life's about trying exciting things . . . and I guess I've always been trying."

"Well, a child can find many ways to keep himself amused, can't he? And adults too. Tell me, Jerry, what were your parents like?"

"My parents were the greatest. My mom, tall and thin; my dad, short and round. Walking down the street they looked like a perfect 10. In life, they were. Mom, strong, ever dignified, always kind. Dad, bright, funny, a driving workaholic. Both gave everything they had for my sister, Evelyn, and me. Their life was a movie in itself. They were German Jews. They met in prewar Berlin and married there in a secret ceremony—because Jews

Mom (left) and Dad (right).

weren't supposed to marry in public. So behind drawn shades and before a few loved ones, they exchanged their vows—'for better or worse, till death do us part.' Under the most trying of circumstances, they kept their vows.

"Many of their relatives soon fled Germany. It was getting ugly. Hitler was clamping down. But for reasons I'll apparently never know, Mom and Dad hung in, until finally, in August of thirty-nine—two weeks before Hitler invaded Poland, starting World War II—they escaped to England. Their mothers stayed behind, which would prove to be a fatal decision. They would never be seen again. They, along with Dad's brother Kurt, were exterminated in the concentration camps. So now my parents, in their midthirties, their families gone, their country gone, their

My grandmother, Marie Kallmann (left). My father's mother, Selma Springer (center). My father's brother, Kurt Springer.

world gone, suddenly found themselves in a strange land, with a strange language, with no choice but to start life over again.

"Obviously, the Holocaust became the defining moment in my family's life. From it emanated our values, our philosophy, and our priorities. It's pretty difficult, after experiencing what prejudice and discrimination can do, to ever tolerate a discriminating act again—no matter at whom it's directed.

"Certainly it'd be nice if it were no longer an issue. And if we choose to, at least for a while, I guess we could pretend that racism no longer exists—that racists are now a mere footnote to history. But I've made it a point on '*The Jerry Springer Show*' not to ignore the existence of these ignorant people in our world. Indeed, we often produce shows involving racists, anti-Semites, Klan members, and other discriminating groups and their leaders. I think they're important shows to do. In fact, there's one I'll never forget.

"It was a show about parents raising their kids to be racists. We do these 'race' shows from time to time and critics fairly ask, Why? Why give these Klan and neo-Nazi-type crazies airtime?

"I've thought about that quite a bit, but there's a good reason. Our show is about outrageousness—those things that are either abnormal or outside the bounds of cultural acceptability. Surely racism fits that description. But I also think it's important to expose this cancer in our society every time we spot it so people will see how evil and crazy and downright stupid it is.

"We can't blame television for spreading racism. It's only when it's ignored or covered up that racism will grow unchallenged. Remember, six million Jews were exterminated in the '30s and '40s by Hitler, and not one person on earth had a television set.

"During the first half of this century African-Americans were regularly lynched from trees in the South—and nobody had a television. Indeed, it was only when the media started to expose and focus in on this horror that we as a society started on the road to eliminating it. We can't stop now.

"Believe me, I find no comfort in talking to neo-Nazis (particularly since the Nazis killed my family), but here in America I believe only when we expose all ideas and all lifestyles will those that are evil fall of their own weight. Justice Brandeis said, 'Sunlight is the greatest disinfectant.' I believe that. Turn on the 'lights, camera . . . action'—bring on the Klan.

"Now, having said that, the one time I actually lost my cool during a taping was, in fact, during an encounter with a racist. The show was called, 'A Racist Family.' The family leader was Rev. August Creis. He's a rather big man in both stature and presence. He has red hair and a beard. He started taunting me by making fun of my mother. He spent much of the show denying the Holocaust and referring to me as a hook-nosed Jew bastard. Finally, he went too far when he made a reference to my mother being turned into a lampshade and tossed into the trunk

Those Klansmen, on their own, are not at all frightening. Their ridiculous beliefs defeat themselves. But when they pass their hatred on to their children, then it's scary.

of a car. I threw my microphone down on the ground and ran up onstage. I was shaking my finger at this guy and I was right in his face, saying, 'Shut your fucking face!'

"Suddenly, Creis stood up and I thought to myself, 'Oh no, now I'm gonna get it.' But obviously I couldn't stand there and let him say those kinds of things about my own mom. Thankfully the security guys leaped in, threw him to the ground, and only when they had him firmly in their grasp did I then jockey around, grunting, 'Let me at him, let me at him!' praying they wouldn't, and thanking God they didn't.

"Ultimately this incident was edited out of the final show. But the audience went crazy over my response. The fact is, I couldn't help it."

"So your grandparents, uncle, and other relatives were killed in the camps, but your parents got out just two weeks before the war started. Is that right?"

"That's right. They fled Germany and made it to England. In London, my dad went right to work. He got a job making uniforms for the English army and always worried that they'd lose the war because he didn't know what he was doing. He kept making the uniforms too snug—making it difficult for the British soldiers to lift their arms. Thankfully, they found someone to fix the problem.

"Pops also worked as an air raid warden, where he would go up on the rooftop of our building with nothing more than a hat and a whistle to signal incoming bombs. He always spoke of that experience with great pain. He would keep a watchful eye, always hoping that the bombs would fall just a little farther away from where he was standing. He didn't want to lose his family,

 Age 2, still living in London.

JERRY SPRINGER

but obviously he always felt bad when the neighbors got it. That's when he decided to send my mother, my sister, and me to a farm near Stratford, England. It was actually an Italian prisoner of war camp, but it was rather civilized. Many women and children stayed at this farm during the war years for their own protection, and my family was no exception. We finally returned to London after the war and lived in apartment #48 at Belvedere Ct. on Littleton Road until 1949.

"A few years ago I was in London promoting my show, and I decided to go back to that apartment for the first time since we had left for America, nearly fifty years earlier. Betsy Bergman, head of affiliate relations for *"The Jerry Springer Show,"* was traveling with me, as she often does. Anyway, we walked up the four flights of stairs and I knocked on the door of the apartment. These very nice people answered the door and I explained that I had lived in their apartment in the 1940s. I asked if I could come in and take a look around. They were only too gracious. They were so nice as they showed us around this tiny flat I had once called 'home.' But as I looked around, something seemed wrong to me. Everything felt backwards. I had remembered it totally the opposite as it appeared. But I just chalked it up to my failing memory and decided I had it wrong in my head. It was great visiting this place of my early youth, even if it wasn't the way I remembered it.

"Last year, I went back to London with my sister and again I said, 'Come on, let's go see the apartment.' She said, 'Okay,' and off we went. Again we climbed the four flights of stairs, and I started heading toward apartment 45, where I *thought* we had lived. In her best inquisitive voice, Evelyn said to me, 'Gerald, what are you doing? We lived *across* the hall—in apartment #48!' Well, at least that explained why everything was flip-flopped.

"So anyway, we knocked on *that* door and these people were also very nice, but residents of that building must be wondering who is this guy who keeps coming back every year knocking on people's doors, telling them he used to live there. I think they're on the lookout for me. They must think I'm a lunatic!"

"Well, we'll be the judge of that. Listen, Jerry, we have to take a commercial break, but when we come back, tell us all about your trip to America, okay?"

"Hey, it's your show. . . . "

"All right then. I'm God, and you're watching my show. Don't change that dial . . . 'cause I'm watching you! We'll be right back!"

So am I supposed to talk to him in between breaks? I mean, David Letterman hates talking during commercials. Jeezel, what's the protocol up here?

"You're doing great, Jerry. I've been looking for a sidekick . . . you know, my own 'Ed McMahon . . . ' but he's not available . . . yet. Maybe we could work something out?"

"I'm not sure I'm going to be around . . . or am I?" (Looking at the monitor, I see the following commercial):

Commercial:

You're dead. Face it. After a lifetime of watching what you eat, looking both ways before crossing the street, and waiting half an hour before you go back into the pool after eating, you're dead. But there is a bright side. Here at "the Burning Bush," Heaven's premier smoke shop and cigar bar, we've created an atmosphere where earth's bad habits become your guiltless pleasures. Run in the house with scissors? You betcha. Caffeine and sugar? Not a problem! And smoking? It's not only permitted, it's encouraged! So stop by "the Burning Bush" and shed your earthly inhibitions. You've waited a lifetime for this!

"Hey, we're back and we're talking with famed talk show meister Jerry Springer. . . . So tell us about your journey to America as a young boy."

"Actually, I left when I found out I couldn't be king! I think Bob Hope said that first!"

"Who's Bob Hope?"

"Oh, you'll meet him one day. He's so funny, you wouldn't believe it.

"Anyway, back to when I came over to America. It was 1949. My mother had a sister who was living in New York, and though this meant that my parents were facing starting their lives over for a third time, in their hearts they felt that moving to America was best for us as a family.

Me and my sis.

"My parents had been waiting to get the proper paperwork for all of us to come over for several years. Once they were able to secure all of the documentation, we sailed on the *Queen Mary*, which took five days. My sister and I didn't even know that we were leaving for America until my mother had taken us shopping to get warm sweaters and jackets for the journey. It was the saleswoman who let it slip. She wished my mother a safe voyage to America. My sister looked up and asked my mother if it was true . . . and she confirmed that we were indeed headed to the 'land of opportunity.'

"She hadn't told us of the plans prior to this because she didn't want to get our hopes up just in case it didn't work out. Another reason we didn't really know a lot about what was going on with my parents is that they spoke very little English. When

Mom and Dad communicated, it was mostly in their native German. As children, we thought that *all* parents spoke this 'double Dutch' language. As children we would play 'grown up,' and Evelyn and I would just speak gibberish. One thing my parents did insist on was that my sister and I speak to them in English so that they could learn the language and be more prepared when we finally made our journey to America.

"We came to America under the Displaced Person's Act of 1948. We had already registered our immigration paperwork in England, so we didn't have to go through the political red tape of entering America via Ellis Island. The memory of sailing into New York harbor early that cold January morning is still quite vivid in my mind. It was the absolute silence I remember as the ship sailed past the Statue of Liberty. In time . . . the promise of her inscription became extremely relevant to me. Years later I remember writing my commentary on this as a broadcaster."

Commentary on the Statue of Liberty, Aired July 3, 1986

A five year old could perhaps be forgiven for not understanding the full significance of the moment . . . which is what I was when Mom awakened me from an afternoon nap. "Come on, Gerald," she said. "We're going up on deck . . . we're going to see the Statue of Liberty . . . we're in America."

And there we stood . . . my parents, sister, and I, along with virtually everyone else on the *Queen Mary* . . . gazing quietly at the first visible evidence of a New World. It's funny what you remember of such moments . . . but what I remember most was the absolute silence of it all. Thousands of us crammed together

Trying to understand that there was no school dress code here in America became a valuable lesson. Every day my mother put me in shorts, knee-high socks, a blazer and tie. I would inevitably come home from school bruised and disheveled from being bullied by the kids. Finally, my mother called one of the neighbors to ask their advice on what I should do to fit in a little better. What my mother took away from that discussion was that in America . . . baseball was everything.

"So she took me to Gertz's department store and bought me a baseball uniform. It happened to be of the New York Yankees. I had no idea what it was (we didn't have baseball in England), but when I wore it, nobody beat me up.

"I soon was afraid to go to school without it. It became my protection, my ticket to acceptance, and soon, my love. To this day, I still love the Yankees.

"My sister often kids around about how as a young child, I could do sports commentating for any event. She remembers that I could recite word for word the broadcast of boxing matches and baseball games. I would listen to Mel Allen do the Yankee games, and I would impersonate him . . . poorly. And when we got our first television set, I would turn the volume off during a ball game and give a play-by-play description of the action. I memorized every statistic from the back of my baseball card collection. Evelyn says this was 'all part of the Americanization of Gerald.'

"Whatever, my life growing up in Queens was pretty normal. When we first arrived in America, we lived in a residential hotel called the Whitehall. And a year later, my parents moved into the Roger Williams apartment building, where they would reside for 32 years.

"My father worked as a salesman, hawking stuffed animals

My parents, after my father sold his business in 1970.

all over the eastern seaboard, and my mother got a job working as a clerk in the mortgage department of a Wall Street bank, where she worked for 23 years. Dad, ever resourceful, grew his business into a nice-sized toy manufacturing company. His biggest selling item was his Emmett Kelly clown doll. Dad finally sold his business when he was in his seventies.

"We weren't rich by any means, but we were an extremely close and comfortable family. We lived in a quiet, safe neighborhood in a time where families looked after each other.

"As a boy, I played stickball in the street and, whenever there wasn't snow, basketball and roller hockey after school with my best buddies. To this very day, my five best friends growing up—Milton, David, John, Billy, and Ronny—are still a vivid part of my memories. We were together every day of our childhood, but once we graduated from college we lost touch. Then,

Another sport I wasn't good at.

Playing hoops with my best friends from PS 99 at my fortieth birthday party thrown for me by my sister, Evelyn.

for my fortieth birthday, my sister, Evelyn, threw a surprise party for me. When I got to her home in Virginia, I was saying hello to some of her guests and I suddenly saw a guy who looked awfully familiar. 'Oh, my God, that's Milton.' And as I was hugging him, I saw John. . . . And only when I went through three or four of them did it dawn on me that this was a surprise party for me.

"Evelyn had found them all after 22 years. It was the greatest weekend. We did 'the Big Chill' thing. I bought sneakers for all the guys, and we spent the next two days playing basketball in the school yard reminiscing—reverting back to our original personalities. Life was never sweeter. It was so much fun that for my fiftieth birthday I invited them all back to New York to do it all over again. I hope I make it to sixty. The boys from PS 99—what wonderful friends."

TWO
Coming into My Own

Meanwhile . . . Back on God's Talk Show . . .

"Well, Jerry, your childhood sounds so normal, I almost can't believe it's you! I mean, how does a shlub from Queens go on to become one of the most talked about and controversial figures in the history of television?"

"Aw, shucks, God, you flatter me. I'm not sure I have a clear explanation. Surely, I never *planned* to become the titan of trash. In fact, I thought that my only two choices growing up were either to become a doctor or a lawyer. Basically, anything that came with initials after my name would do. I never expected those initials to be SOB."

"So was college the beginning of your decline?"

"College was perfect. It's really when I started to come into my own. I won a New York State Regents Scholarship, so I could have gone to any college in New York and had my tuition and expenses paid for. But my parents, God love them, knew what

This is when I graduated from junior high school. I didn't let anyone stand next to me so no one could see how short I was.

was best for my development. They, with the encouragement of my sister, thought it was best that I go out of town.

"I should tell you . . . virtually every person from my graduating class went on to college. You see, I grew up in a pretty good neighborhood, where there was an emphasis on education. It wasn't a rich neighborhood, but it was a smart neighborhood. It was very European, with a strong work ethic and a great emphasis on learning. Now my high school was huge—5,000 kids, 1,201 in the graduating class—and with so many students going on to college, it couldn't process all of the paperwork fast enough, so we were limited to five applications. I decided that I would apply to one college in every part of the country. New Orleans seemed like a cool place . . . the South intrigued me, what with the civil rights movement and everything, and politics was already a part of my blood. So I decided upon Tulane University in New Orleans.

"My political interests had started at home because every night at dinner, for as long as I can remember, we had to talk about something that was in the newspaper that day. Politics was cherished in my home growing up, I suppose due to the lack of political freedom my parents had experienced so early in their lives. I remember as a family we would stay up all night watching the political conventions.

"In fact, I vividly recall the '56 political conventions. I remember there was a fight over the vice presidency. This new senator from Massachusetts, John Kennedy, was being nominated for vice president and he ended up giving a speech saying that he'd decided to pull out, withdrawing and giving his support to Estes Kefauver. Even then he seemed incredibly impressive.

"Anyway, 1960, my senior year, was the year of the Kennedy-Nixon race. It was late into election night, and the results were still undecided. My family and I stayed up all night watching the returns, until finally we knew there would be no answer until the following day.

"The next morning, Evelyn and I had to start getting ready for school and my parents for work, and none of us had been to sleep. My mother never, ever missed a day of work in the 23 years she worked as a clerk at the bank. Consequently, we were never allowed to miss a day of school.

"Mom says to us that morning, 'Okay, kids. We've got to go to work and you both have school.' My dad says, 'Yeah. Everybody's got to go to work. Everybody's got to go to school.' But my sister and I resisted, citing that 'there are still three states out.' (I think it was Illinois, California, and Texas.)

"Anyway, knowing we were never going to win this battle, we begrudgingly got dressed and left. Thinking it was safe to head out, Mom left for work, comfortable in her mind that we were all also on our way. At the time, Evelyn was attending Queens College. She headed for school and I took the subway to Forest Hills High School. At the first subway stop, I said to myself, 'I'm cutting school.' So I got off the train, got to the other side of the platform, and made my way home. When I opened the door, there was Evelyn. She had come back to watch too. So we were laughing and thinking we were totally getting away with this. Ten minutes later, there was a key in the door, and we thought to ourselves in a panic, 'Oh, my God.' But in walked Pop. He had come back, too. So the three of us were sitting there in front of our television, basking in our truancy. Finally, at ten in the morning I think, Nixon conceded and—and Kennedy was our president. Mom, of course, stayed at work. We 'fessed up to her later that night.

This is one of my favorite pictures of me with my parents.

"I tell that story because it really is a barometer of how important politics was and still is to me and it's impacted just about every facet of my life. It certainly was a factor in my choosing Tulane.

"My trip down to New Orleans was my first real brush with civil rights and the issues of equality. It was September 5, 1961. I took a propeller plane to Atlanta, where you had to change planes to get to New Orleans. At least that part hasn't changed.

"I got off the plane in Atlanta. I was so nervous, being away from home and flying for the first time, I was afraid I would miss my connection. I rushed through the airport and stopped at a water fountain for a drink. There was a much longer line on one, so I decided to use the one next to it, which had no line at all.

"As I'm drinking from this other fountain, a guy grabs me from the back of the neck and pulls me away because it said 'Colored' over it. He started screaming at me, and I was terrified. I didn't know what was going on. I looked up and there was another sign over the adjoining fountain that read 'White.' I was just thirsty, and coming from New York, I guess I just hadn't had to deal with this issue. I remember walking away, hoping that this wasn't how my whole stay in the South would be. But it was a different time and there would, in fact, be other incidents that would mold my position, politically speaking, on civil rights.

"Of course, politics wasn't the only thing on my mind on the eve of my Tulane experience. I remember being scared the night before I left for college, and I spoke of it years later on the air while doing commentary on WLWT in Cincinnati."

Going to College,
Aired September 4–5, 1986

I remember the first time I left for college. I remember, the night before I left, thinking more about what I was leaving than what lay ahead. At the age of 17 I knew pitifully little about life, but I knew enough to know that when I left home the following morning, it would never be the same. I would still love my parents, but it'd be by letter and phone. The guys on the block with whom I grew up, with whom I spent 12 years playing ball in the school yard (and sharing lies about girls we were too scared to ask out), these friends that are friends as only kids can be friends, all this was about to change, and I knew it.

I didn't sleep much that last night at home, staring at my pennants from camp and mementos from school, my walls plastered with pictures of the Yankees, cars, and Annette Funicello, with Annette getting most of the attention. For I knew once the morning came and I left my room for the life of college, things would never be the same. And I'm not sure I liked the idea. Indeed, in the privacy of my room, I was scared to death and I cried. But the tears were for naught, for college became life's finest moment. It was an invitation to test the world, to learn about it, and to shape it.

Today that seems pretty naïve, but this was 1961, and all was possible. At least that's what we thought. Our imagination was our only limitation. A president, who looked as young as we did, spoke to us of new frontiers and shared burdens, and we bought the whole package.

But our puritanical social conscience was tempered by a less than serious view of campus life. We were the last generation of collegians that could listen to Peter, Paul, and Mary and

Frankie Avalon and not be embarrassed. Fraternities were "in," campus violence was a panty raid, and college football was king. We were the last class before the loss of innocence. By the time we graduated, our president would be shot, our campuses would be in turmoil, our cities would burn, and Vietnam would bury our classmates. College, much like life, would never be the same.

Now, perhaps those who started college today aren't so scared. Perhaps they didn't cry last night, and maybe for a good reason. A quarter of a century later, we're running out of shocks. For better or worse, today's 17 year olds are already aware of how the world lives, of the pain it shares, and of the damage we can do to each other. Maybe that's why incoming freshmen seem so much older today. I hope they'll be as happy.

"Landing in New Orleans was an incredible week of my life. How I love New Orleans.

"My first week at Tulane was fraternity 'Rush Week'—a parade of parties where fraternities decide which freshmen they will offer bids. Hopefully, you don't get shut out. I was pretty much of a geek and was prepared for the worst. But luckily I got a bid from Tau Epsilon Phi. I didn't know much about this fraternity stuff at the time, and apparently neither did my parents. But I knew it was a great way to meet people, and I wanted to be a part of it all. Who wouldn't, I thought. In fact, when I landed in New Orleans, there to greet me were 25 guys, all representing different fraternities, grabbing my luggage. 'Come with us. We'll take you to the dorm.' And off we went. We stopped there long enough to drop off my bags—and then it was off to the French Quarter. Let the partying begin.

"*Every* night the fraternity brothers took us down to Bourbon

"Well, to be honest, I don't think I was thinking about my future at the time."

"In any event, I loved Tulane. I did really well, and for the first time, I had a social life. I had girlfriends. I was falling in love every night. . . . Everything just clicked at college. I was a very small kid going in—about 5'2". All of the sudden I just shot up. Today I'm 6'0".

"I was getting involved with tons of school activities, too. I became involved in Campus Night, which was the annual school musical. The year I participated was an original show called '298 B.C., or How Much Can a Grecian Urn?' I played Alexander the Lesser. I wore a toga and actually had to sing. We even cut an album, which was full of all of the original show music! (It's probably worth $2.98 if you have a copy of it today!)

"I was also becoming increasingly more politically active. I participated in the demonstrations to integrate the high school in New Orleans in '61, and got involved with a lot of civil rights stuff. We'd take bus rides into Mississippi to try and register blacks to vote. I became obsessed with the whole civil rights movement. I really do believe my parents ingrained in me an inherent sense of justice. I don't think you can be a child of the Holocaust and not have that hot button when it comes to any issue of discrimination. I never even had to think about it. It *was* and *remains* in my blood."

"But, Jerry, if politics was so important to you back then, why did you end up in show business? You ought to be sitting on Capitol Hill voting on a bill or debating William Bennett. But instead, you wrangle a gang of crazies for a living. Why do you suppose that is?"

"You see, God, it's like this. The talk show is my job. I love it. It's great fun to do, I meet fascinating people, it pays well, it'll provide for my daughter forever, but it doesn't define my politics or my religion or my values.

"It's just a job. What a person does for a living doesn't determine what he or she believes or thinks. If someone drives a truck, does that mean he's not religious or isn't a good parent or doesn't love his country? No. It's what he does to put food on the table.

"I haven't changed my political views or values because I do this show. I didn't sell out and suddenly become a conservative. I'm as liberal and as committed to the underdog as I've ever been."

"Well, is there a connection between show business and politics?"

"I remember the first time those two paths crossed for me. It was purely coincidental, but, you see, at the time I was a noon-time DJ on this hole-in-the-wall campus radio station, WTUL. It was November 22, 1963, and I was playing Elvis Presley's 'Don't Be Cruel' when the bells rang on the Teletype. Back then we had no computers, all of the news came over the Teletype.

"And, sure enough, the ticker said that shots had been fired at the presidential motorcade in Dallas. And then, a few minutes later, the tickertape said that the president had been hit. I wasn't going to go on the radio and say that, especially because I didn't even know if it was true. I assumed it was a joke. The president's shot. What kind of garbage is that? But the news kept coming, and I figured, 'Oh, shit. It must be true!' So I ran across the hall and into the yearbook office, where they had a black and white

TV. I said, 'Turn on the TV.' And, sure enough, there's Walter Cronkite talking about the president having been killed. It was just devastating.

"So I went back to the radio station and informed all of my listeners (or, more accurately, both of my listeners) to 'turn on your television; the president's been shot.' And all I could do from that point on was put the station on automatic classical music and head back to my room, where I spent the next four days—like the rest of America—watching.

"We would never be the same."

"Anyway, I remember Tulane and New Orleans and those college years with great fondness—indeed, wonderful life experiences. I'd do it all again in a heartbeat.

"Incidentally, I have been back a few times recently—as a speaker at their homecoming and also the grand marshal of one of the parades at '98 Mardi Gras. In fact, it was at this event that I finally realized that people knew me. Even my security was amazed. Steve Wilkos and Todd Schultz were there with me at the time, and Todd remembers it like this":

Todd Schultz,
STAGE MANAGER/SECURITY 1994–PRESENT

I never thought I would get sick of the "Jer-ry! Jer-ry!" chanting. That was before I went down to New Orleans with Jerry when he was one of the grand marshals of Mardi Gras. Six miles and four hours down the parade route, I didn't hear anything else. We were supposed to ride in a convertible in front of Jerry's float, but there were so many people throwing beads and empty cups at the float, Steve Wilkos and I had to ride on the float with Jerry for his own protection.

After the parade we made the mistake of going to Bourbon Street, which was a total mob scene. The street is usually jammed, but at least the crowds move along down the street. But so many people wanted to talk with Jerry, it was at a standstill. Eventually, we got invited up to a balcony off the street. So we hung out up there until the cops showed up and asked if Jerry would please go inside because nobody was moving on the street. Jerry went inside, but nobody left—the crowd still chanting "Jer-ry! Jer-ry! Jer-ry!" He spent the rest of his trip confined to his room.

"This was a wild trip—but clearly, I was no longer one of the guys. My hanging out days were over. College was a distant memory."

"So you really weren't crazy about becoming a lawyer?"

"No. My passion was politics: civil rights, the antiwar movement. I guess I just saw law as a way to make a living."

"How did you get to Cincinnati?"

"Well, I was in my second year of law school, and it was a gray, cold Chicago November afternoon. On the bulletin board, coming out of one of my classes, I noticed that there was an interview being held by this large corporate law firm in Cincinnati, Ohio, for summer internships. I just happened to see it. I thought about it for a minute, and I realized I didn't have any plans for the summer. So I casually wrote down the information and stuffed it in my pocket. I remember I kept asking myself, 'Cincinnati?' The only thing I knew about Cincinnati was that they'd lost to the Yankees in '61.

"Whatever, I decided to go to the interview anyway. I walked in late, wearing a sweatshirt and jeans, while these guys were all in their three-piece suits. This was Frost and Jacobs, Cincinnati's largest firm. They seemed to represent everyone: the *Cincinnati Enquirer*, the gas and electric company, the telephone company, the Reds, the Bengals. It was **THE** firm. And boy, were they conservative.

"My guess is they'd never had a Democrat, nor do I believe they'd ever had a Jew working there. They certainly had never had a liberal, and here I was a war protestor. I could not have been what they were looking for. I wasn't trying to candy coat anything. I would say things like, 'Yep. I love Bobby Kennedy.' And, 'We've got to get out of the war; it's horrible.' I mean, I was this pinko lefty, a total liberal. I remember thinking that was the end of the interview, and there was no way they were going to hire me. I walked out and just put it out of my mind.

"So, a month later it's Christmas vacation, and I'm back in New York. I was at my parents' apartment, sick with the flu, and the telephone rings. Mom knocks on the door, says, 'Gerald, it's for you.'

" 'Hello. This is John Egbert.'

"It was the phone call that changed my life. He was the partner who'd conducted the interview—and unbelievably offered me an internship for the summer. If it wasn't for that phone call, I wouldn't have gone to Cincinnati; I wouldn't have met Micki and had Katie. I wouldn't have become Cincinnati's mayor—and then been offered a job to anchor the news there. If I hadn't done that, I wouldn't have gotten this job as talk show host. All of this because of one interview, one phone call. Thank God the line wasn't busy.

"Anyway, I accepted the internship. So at the end of the school year, I packed up my old Studebaker, my first car, and headed to Ohio. That old car had 100,000 miles on it, and the brakes were terrible. I had to pump them or the car wouldn't stop.

"Now it's June 11, 1967. I arrive in Cincinnati on a Sunday evening. And I have absolutely no idea where to go. I've never been here before. I didn't have a place to live. I see a sign off the highway that says UNIVERSITY OF CINCINNATI, so I figured there'll be a lot of young people around. I'll find a place to live there.

"I stop into this bar called Duffs. I go up to the bartender and notice there's a whole crowd gathered around, staring at the TV. Ever oblivious, I say, 'Hi. I've just arrived in town. I'm looking for a place to live. Can you make any recommendations?' But everyone's focused on the screen. The bartender says to me, 'I'm sorry, I can't help you. You're gonna have to leave. We have to close down. There's a curfew.'

"Sunday, June 11, 1967. It's the night of the riots in Cincinnati. *Just my luck.* I had just arrived in town, and maybe they weren't too happy to see me, but why riot?"

"Obviously, Jerry, wherever you go there's a fight!"

"Very funny, God. I have to assume it's some cruel practical joke you enjoy playing on me. But meanwhile, back in Cincinnati, I get back into the car and I'm desperately trying to figure out a way to leave town. I drive down the street and I make a left at the first major light. It was just the wrong turn to make; I headed right into the heart of the riots.

"They're shooting. They're rock throwing, screaming and yelling. All of a sudden a cop came over and told me to pull over to the curb, turn off the ignition, and get under my steering wheel. I vividly remember huddling there with my head covered, and I could hear all of this screaming and yelling going on outside. And I'm thinking to myself, *What's going on?* Here I've just arrived in Cincinnati. I've never even heard of the place. There's a riot going on. Everything I own is in this car. *What am I doing here?*

"A few minutes later there's banging on the window and I look up, thinking somebody's trying to break in. But, thankfully, it was a cop. He says, 'Come out of there, kid. I'll take you home.' I explained to him that I had no place to go. So that first night they put me up at the downtown YMCA.

"The next morning I went into Frost and Jacobs, and all I had to say to my new bosses was, 'Nice town!'

"Anyway, a few days later I found an apartment and quickly started sinking my teeth into the practice of law, or so I thought.

"Working at the firm was a really good experience. Everyone was extremely nice. From the beginning they knew my politics were different. They supported my political ambition. I think they saw me as somewhat of an oddity, but I did good work for them, and that's what mattered.

"It was while I was there that I decided to run for Congress, in 1970, as an antiwar candidate."

"Weren't you a little young to be getting so involved in politics, Jerry?"

"I didn't think so. In 1968, I worked on Robert Kennedy's presidential campaign for three months, which was so exciting for me because I really thought he was our only realistic hope of getting us out of Vietnam. That experience ignited what was to become the political fire in my belly.

"So in 1969 I headed up this campaign to lower the voting age to 19. At that time you still had to be 21 to vote. It was before the twenty-sixth constitutional amendment. That was really my first political activity in Cincinnati, and though the referendum to lower the voting age lost statewide, our campaign was successful locally. It passed overwhelmingly, and coincidentally, it launched my political career. You see, during the campaign I had given a speech at a Democratic fund-raising dinner, arguing that those old enough to fight in this war ought to be able to vote. After all, who had more of a stake in political decisions than these young men and women who were putting their lives on the line?

"Sen. Birch Bayh, who was head of the Senate Judiciary

 Guidelines that ultimately ratified the Twenty-sixth Amendment.

Committee, was in attendance that night. And he heard my talk. It was my first major speech, and it really got a good reception. Afterward, all of the bigwigs in attendance came up and started talking to me about my goals and aspirations. I was pretty fed up with the war—actively participating in demonstrations—and indicated to them that *if* I was going to get involved, the war would be the issue.

"I started thinking about Congress. I picked the most conservative district in Ohio. It was the western half of Cincinnati and Hamilton County and the congressman there was a fellow named Don Clancy, who was a long-time congressman. He was the favorite son, but very Republican, very conservative. And he was the ranking member of the Armed Services Committee. So I figured this was a perfect person to run against, because I was a dove and he was a hawk. So on November 25, 1969, I announced my candidacy for the U.S. Congress.

"Understand, I'm only 25. And I've only been living in Cincinnati for six months. It was one of these things where everyone was saying, 'Who's he?' But I figured it didn't matter. The war and where it was taking us was what was important to me. It just seemed to be purely a politician's war—a war that never made any sense. It was clear, whether we were winning the war or losing it, that at some point, even if we won, we would eventually have to bring everybody home. And as soon as we did that—being in the backyard of China and the Soviet Union—Vietnam would all turn Communist again, which, of course, is exactly what happened. So what was the point? Why were we sending all of our sons to die?

"As I said, I announced my candidacy for Congress. I was going to be an antiwar candidate. Well, not so fast. On Friday,

November 28, three days later, I had all my hair shaven off as I was called up on active duty in the Army Reserves. I was a lawyer in the army—but I still had to go to boot camp.

"Now Don Clancy, who I was running against, was on the Armed Services Committee. So I used to joke about how my notice to report to active duty came so conveniently and immediately after I announced that I was running against him. Whatever—campaign or no campaign—I was off to Fort Knox for basic training.

"I didn't tell anyone down there that I was a candidate for Congress, because I didn't want any problems. Needless to say, we basically put the campaign on an immediate halt.

"Virtually all the guys in boot camp with me were 18 years old, getting ready, sadly for them, to go to Vietnam. I was 25, never having done a knee bend in my life. So basic training was physically challenging for me. Just in terms of culture, it was a shock from being in the midst of a major law firm, starting off a race for U.S. Congress, and now all of a sudden I'm doing push-ups in the mud. Which, of course, in retrospect, was nothing compared to the rest of the guys, who were wondering whether they would live or die in Vietnam.

"I remember arriving at boot camp our first night. We were all sitting in this big room and had to fill out a slew of forms. It was just tons of paperwork. They asked us, 'How many of you have finished high school?' and about half the guys raised their hands. Next question . . . 'Anyone go to college?' And out of the 500 guys in the room, four had been to college. 'Anyone go beyond college?' they asked. Now I'm the *only* one that had gone beyond college, finishing law school. The drill sergeant said, 'Oh! We got Mr. Einstein here.' So then I was known as 'Mr. Einstein' from that day forward . . . until the Christmas show, of which I was put in charge.

"The drill sergeant came to me and said, 'You organize the Christmas show.' So, since I was organizing the big event, I decided that I would be the MC (master of ceremonies). I opened the show, and I was all loose, telling jokes and entertaining the guys. And then . . . my fatal error. I made a wisecrack about the drill sergeants. I was making fun of their 'Smokey the Bear' hats and how they just beat the crap out of us every day. The final straw came when I said, 'Hey, we got a lot of great acts, and later on, we're gonna have one of the drill sergeants come up here and do an impersonation of a human being.' Of course, the guys thought it was real funny, but not the sergeants.

"The next morning, reveille sounded at three in the morning instead of the usual four-thirty. Once we heard reveille, we had two minutes to get dressed and report outside to the sergeant on duty. It was a freezing cold December morning, and we were all standing at attention.

"Not saying a word at first, the sergeant stood one by one in front of every guy and screamed, 'Are you a dickhead?' And each guy down the line said, 'No, sir!' This went on for every guy in my group. 'Are you a dickhead?' 'No, sir!' Finally he got to me and said, ' Are you a dickhead?' And I said, 'No, sir!' but he didn't move. He barked at me again, 'I said, are you a dickhead?' Uh-oh, maybe I am. So I responded, 'Yes, sir?' And he said, 'Okay, Private Dickhead, you're going to do an impersonation of a soldier. Gimme a hundred—now' (which meant pushups). The whole company was out there freezing until I completed a hundred. I thought the war would end first. But from then on, in the army I was 'Dickhead!'

"That is until the day my commanding officer called me into his office. Apparently he had been given the information that I was actively seeking political office, and Sen. Birch Bayh had personally requested that I come to Washington, D.C., to testify in front of the Senate Judiciary Committee on behalf of lowering the voting age. So with that, I was off to Washington, returning to my passion, and once again, and for the first time in months, being referred to as *'Private Springer.'*

"I eventually won the Democratic primary, where I ran against a man named Vernon Bible. As it turned out, he was ineligible anyway, because he had voted in a Republican primary within the past four years. In any event, it wasn't easy to run against a man named 'Bible,' particularly in this conservative district. And what about the headline—'SPRINGER SLASHES BIBLE.' I hope you weren't angry with me, God."

"Why do you think I had you lose the general election?"

"Actually, it was a very close race—and because of my showing, my political career in Cincinnati was launched."

FOUR
Wine, Women, & Politics

Special News Bulletin

We interrupt our regularly scheduled program to bring you the following news bulletin from earth. New York City mayor Rudy Giuliani has announced that he is close to finalizing a deal to take over the hosting responsibilities for the *"The Jerry Springer Show."* Springer, who died yesterday at age fifty-four, went out as the number-one-rated show.

Giuliani, best known as the mayor who "cleaned up" New York, follows in the footsteps of Jerry Springer, himself a former mayor. May. Ed Koch, who now hosts his own courtroom television show, was not available for comment.

Speculation on what kinds of changes Giuliani would make to *"The Jerry Springer Show"* can only be based on the significant impact he has had on New York City. During his reign, Giuliani has shut down sex shops, cleaned up the once sleaze-infested Times Square, and forcibly instilled a dress code for New York cabbies and insisted, at the risk of being fined, that they be "polite." It's likely he'll clean up the show, but when contacted for comment, all Giuliani would say was, "Call me RU-DY! RU-DY!"

We'll keep you updated on any further developments as they come in. We now return you to your regularly scheduled programming.

"Okay . . . we're back. I'm G☉D, and we're still talking with Jerry Springer."

"Uh, God, we have to talk. I know that you have this master plan, but Rudy Giuliani? He'll blow all of our hard work. He's a fine mayor, but what does he know about hosting a talk show?"

"Well, isn't that an interesting question—especially coming from you, Jerry! I mean, how hypocritical can you get? Weren't you once a big city mayor?"

"Well, yes, I was Cincinnati's mayor—but I did other things too."

"Well, we'll get to that—but first, tell us about your political career."

"Well, I already told you about my race for Congress, but we haven't yet talked about my years in city council. But, God . . . if we go there . . . can you find it in your heart to make a decision regarding my fate? I can't let Giuliani take over my show."

"I will give you my decision after you explain your days in office. But, you've got some explaining to do."

"Phew. Okay, here goes . . .

"After I lost my race for Congress in 1970, the media and the politicos immediately started talking about my future. You see, it'd been a real close race. No one had ever gotten that close to my opponent before, so they figured I had some real possibilities. Well, Jack Gilligan had just been elected Ohio governor, and he called me over Thanksgiving asking if I would join his cabinet as state youth director. This was the year of the Kent State killings, and college campuses were hotbeds of controversy everywhere. He thought I might be helpful in putting young people to work in their respective communities. I jumped at the chance. But by springtime, the political leaders in Cincinnati were up visiting me in Columbus, asking if I'd be interested in coming back to Cincinnati to run for city council in a city-wide election. I decided to do it. Politics was now in my blood.

"I won—and on December 1, 1971, my career in public office began. Mike Ford again ran my campaign, as he had the congressional race, and we forged a political bonding and a friendship that has lasted a lifetime. He remains to this day the smartest man I ever met in politics, a wonderful pure soul, and we keep promising ourselves that one day we've got to do it again—not for a job, title, or ego, but for a cause—a purpose for living—and we'll know it when we see it.

"Whatever, my first day on the city council was perhaps a precursor of how controversy would always be a part of my public life. I don't set out to be a troublemaker, but I certainly do seem to attract a lot of heat. I introduced an ordinance, which, if passed, would have prohibited Cincinnati residents from serving in undeclared wars. I was trying to tweak the administration for sending our young men to die in Vietnam when Congress had, in fact, never declared war. President Johnson probably didn't have the votes to do it anymore, and I wanted a test case to be taken immediately to the courts. Not only did the council vote me down 8–1, I was ripped by both Cincinnati newspapers, various radio and TV stations, politicians of all stripes, calling me everything from a traitor to a quack to someone who ought to be paying

My election staff team for Congress with Mike Ford in the middle with me.

attention to city concerns, not international relations. I still think I was right but I was clearly a loose cannon and more than a few folks had to be wondering, 'Oh my God, what have we elected?' "

Mike Ford,
POLITICAL CONSULTANT

Jerry's job as a politician was to be the public passion for the cause—whatever it was. He was the heart of the matter. Jerry Springer was young, but smart enough not to be threatened by his team being smarter than he was. That is rare. In politics, you can't lead if you can't make people follow—and Springer knew how to get people to follow.

Tim Burke, now the chairman of the Democratic Party, and I ran Jerry's campaign. We did it out of love for the guy. We split the salary of $7,000 a year, so it wasn't for the money. We were cramped into this tiny office in City Hall sharing two desks between the three of us. Jerry Springer can make you laugh, cry, or get mad . . . but he always aims to do the right thing, especially when it comes to the community.

"Whatever, I did soon settle down to local issues. Tom Luken, the mayor and my mentor at the time, taught me wonderful lessons about politics and how to serve your constituency. He appointed me head of the ad hoc committee on mass transit. I threw myself into the issue—admittedly a long way from Vietnam—but we did manage to take over the transit system, drop the fare to a quarter, vastly increase service, and perhaps because of that issue and a real connection I was building with voters, I was reelected at the age of twenty-nine—with the second most votes in the city out of twenty people running."

"Politically, I had clearly arrived. The future seemed limitless."

"But something happened, didn't it? Something about a check?"

"Like you don't know. Okay, I'll tell your audience.

"In the early spring of 1974, I was watching the local news and suddenly this story came on about a northern Kentucky health club being shut down because of acts of prostitution.

Decide, and then vote.

Springer
for
Council

issued by Springer for Council, P.W. Barney, Treasurer.

 A flyer from my original campaign for city council.

Specifically, massages were being given that were 'all over massages' . . . before they were all over. I remember being startled. I had been to this club. I had been a customer. Thankfully I wasn't there when it got raided. I thought, *What an idiot I am.*

"Well, a few days later I started getting some anonymous calls at the office: 'We know you were there; you'll be hearing from us.' I was really frightened. I knew I had screwed up badly. I didn't want to spend the rest of my life with this hanging over my head. I didn't want to be blackmailed. I didn't want to drag this thing out either. So I resigned from the city council immediately. The next day I held a press conference announcing why I had done that, explaining my inexcusable behavior.

"The initial reaction was that I had overreacted. By today's standards that may be true. But back then it was a bigger deal; and the truth is, I did feel awful. I felt ashamed. I had hurt people. I just wanted to get my life together. I felt that fessing up immediately and stepping down was the right thing to do.

"Anyway, when the proprietors of that health club went to trial, I became a witness for the prosecution, showing the check I had written as evidence. That became part of Cincinnati folklore. To this day people still make jokes about my stupidity; and while not wanting to pour cold water over this incident that took place over a quarter of a century ago, let me put aside some myths. Let me clear the record once and for all.

"First, I never bounced a check.

"Second, I was never arrested for anything in my life.

"Third, I never had to give up the mayoralty because of a scandal. In fact, I was elected mayor of Cincinnati by the largest plurality in the city's history four years **after** this incident.

"I'm not suggesting that what I did is the right way to become successful in life; but the truth is, it was only *after* my screwup in northern Kentucky that my career finally took off—only *after* that that I went on to become mayor, a candidate for governor, a number-one news anchor for ten years, and now the host of the number-one talk show in America.

"I've been incredibly lucky. The people of Cincinnati were incredibly kind and generous and supportive. I've had a wonderful, charmed life, surely better than any one person deserves. I am forever grateful.

"Anyway, I did come back and run for city council in the next election. It was the toughest race of my life. The campaign was ugly, the party wouldn't endorse me, but—for whatever reason—I won big. As you might expect, I was then welcomed back into the Democratic fold and by the next election, 1977, beat everybody and was elected mayor of Cincinnati—to this day, the single proudest moment of my professional life.

"Please understand the day. In a packed City Hall, with my wife, Micki, and our one-year-old Katie by my side; introduced by council member Charlie Taft, the son of the president; I, the son of Holocaust survivors, myself an immigrant to this country, was sworn in as the mayor of a major American city. Does anyone doubt the promise of America?

"Don't.

"The dream is real."

Mike Ford,
POLITICAL CONSULTANT

Jerry always consistently attracted a certain constituency of voters. The young voters, especially on college campuses,

seemed to flock to him. Of course, he would work the campuses and recruit students to blanket the neighborhoods, knocking door to door, working on his campaign. African-American, lower- to middle-income whites, and the less educated were always part of Jerry's audience. That coalition has certainly transferred into his viewing audience today.

"Anyway, to less serious matters. One of the first things I did as mayor was bring rock concerts to the city. I love music and would often perform myself, singing country tunes and playing my guitar at local bars and coffee houses around Cincinnati. I was able to meet some of my favorite celebrities along the way. You see, the mayor gets to give out the key to the city; so whenever I wanted to meet someone, I'd call up their office and offer them the key. I met Billy Joel, Dolly Parton, Joni Mitchell, Bruce Springsteen, and Bob Dylan. In fact, when the Beach Boys came to town, I got up on stage with them and sang 'Barbara Ann.' I gave out so many keys as mayor that by the end of my term I ran out and had to start giving out the combination: 14 to the right, 7 to the left, 10 to the right.

"Always the Ringmaster, one time the Russian circus came to town. They had a bear that would wrestle. As the mayor, and for charity, I agreed to get into the ring with him. I was told that he wouldn't hurt me unless I swatted him on the nose. So there I am, the reigning political figure of Cincinnati, and I'm wrestling a bear. I start to bob and weave and take a shot here and there, and the bear and I are dancing all over the place. Feeling a little cocky, I bopped him one—right on the nose. The next thing I remember was flying through the air and being pinned by this enormous bear, a welt on the side of my face. Everyone was laughing. I was in pain, afraid, and I couldn't scream or cry

Who says I like fighting?

because this was being televised live. Thank God he was wearing a muzzle. But, once again, a fight breaks out wherever I go. . . .

"Most importantly, being mayor of Cincinnati allowed me the opportunity to do some good. I helped to get health clinics built

in many of the city's lower-income neighborhoods. I helped provide local recreation centers too. I negotiated the end of the transit strike and established the mobile City Hall. Twice a week we took this huge van to a different neighborhood where

To Jerry —
With warm regards!
Dick

My first assignment after losing the primary race for governor: interview my opponent, Richard Celeste.

citizens would come and talk with me and my staff, one on one, about a particular problem they had. Perhaps it was my first talk show, though I don't think anybody threw anything.

"I loved being the mayor. It fulfilled my need to serve in office and to make a change, small as those changes might seem today. It was the most fulfilling job I've ever had. My job today as talk show host is more fun, but being mayor was the most challenging.

"Ultimately, I took a stab at running for governor of the state of Ohio, a race where I would surely be the underdog. While Cincinnati had an idea of who I was, the rest of the state had practically never heard of me. I had a long road ahead of me if I was to pull off this victory. It was a great race, taking me to every part of the state: to the coal mines of northeastern Ohio, to Little Italy in Cleveland, to country clubs in Dayton. What an education. Two months before the election, I pulled to within three points of the lead in the polls.

"Oh, my God. What if we win! But we were now out of money and broke. I lost. Deservedly so. Dick Celeste was at that point more experienced. He deserved to win. I ultimately offered my support to him, spending the rest of my summer campaigning on his behalf. Celeste became the governor of Ohio, and, in an ironic twist of fate, I would interview him on election night as my first assignment for WLWT, the NBC affiliate in Cincinnati, with whom I had signed on to do the news."

"Well, there's an old saying, Jerry. What goes around, comes around—and sometimes it smacks you right in the back of the head. . . . "

"You might have a point there, God."

FIVE
This Just In . . .

"After I lost the race for governor, I decided to go away to Hilton Head for a little rest. While there I received calls from two of the major affiliates in Cincinnati, NBC and ABC. Nick Clooney, George's dad and a well-known news anchor there, called to offer me a job where I would come and do political reporting and commentaries for their news, which was the number-one news at the time. I think he thought that with my background I would attract viewers.

"Channel Five, the NBC affiliate, must have thought so too, because they offered me pretty much the same deal, but they also wanted me to be an anchor. At the time, they were in last place in the ratings.

"Once I got back to Cincinnati, I was also invited to lunch by the CBS affiliate, and they, too, were talking about the possibility of me doing political commentary. So all of a sudden, having absolutely no background in television at all, I'm being courted to do the news, a transition I never anticipated in my career. Why did all of this happen?

"Back in 1976, I had run into Bo Wood. He and his dad were the founders of WEBN, the number-one counterculture rock station in Cincinnati. I was on the city council at the time. He asked me if I'd consider doing a morning commentary of just what's going on in City Hall. My only radio experience was back at Tulane, but it definitely interested me to return to radio.

"So twice a week I did what became known as the 'Springer Memorandum' on WEBN. To my surprise, it was very popular, so they expanded it to three and then four days a week. It became hugely successful. I did these commentaries from 1976 to 1982. They were two-minute commentaries, and they weren't just about politics. I talked about culture, comedy, or some current event that might have been going on either locally or nationally.

"I was getting great reviews, a large audience, and the bigwigs at the station seemed very happy. It's funny though because even though they loved what I had to say on the air, the management knew I was a politician, so they didn't really trust me. They never gave me a key to the studio. I had to get there at seven in the morning and go to the phone booth down the street, ring up Robin Wood, who was Bo's sister and the morning DJ at the time, and ask her to let me in. She would send her sidekick down to open the door. It was a little bit weird because I was already the mayor and I'd been doing these commentaries for six years, yet they still wouldn't let me have my own key. I guess, once you're a politician, you never get the trust back.

"Well, I guess it was the combination of the success of the radio stint—and my following as the mayor—that led the television stations to believe I could be successful as a news anchor. I obviously knew the community and the people knew me. Each of the stations thought it was worth a shot.

"Anyway, I decided to accept the job with the NBC affiliate. I took that job for several reasons. First, because Nick Clooney (with the ABC affiliate) was already the number-one anchor in town. What could I do for him? Second, I figured that if I started across the street at the bottom, I had no place to go but up. And

Empirical proof that I'm a hunka-hunka burnin' love.

third, since not too many people were watching NBC at the time, it would be a good place for me to learn.

"It turned out to be a wonderful ten years that culminated in ten Emmy awards: seven for commentaries and three for best anchor and special reports.

"For me, doing the news was an interesting time in my life. I had never expected to end up in this field; and although it's hardly the toughest job in the world, I did have some memorable experiences and met some wonderful people. I also managed to squeeze in some fun.

"I remember doing a commentary about two months after I had started. January 8, 1983, Elvis Presley's birthday. And being that 'the King' was one of my heroes, I decided to do a commentary about him. At the time, we used old-time

TelePrompTers, where the person working the prompter had to feed the sheet of paper with what I was going to say through the machine. You are completely at the mercy of this person. If he doesn't get the paper down properly, there's nothing in the camera. If he puts the sheets of paper in the wrong order or places them upside down, you're in big trouble, because you're 'live' on the air.

"I wrote down my script on Elvis, and I saw the first page safely going through, and I was just reading along as usual. Well, all of a sudden the next page goes in and it's clearly the wrong one. The TelePrompTer guy also realized this; but I was live, so I had to start improvising. I saw this guy's hand coming through, but no paper, and I was panicking. Then I saw a paper on the prompter. I thought I was saved, but this one was upside down. All I could do was mumble a few words. And all of a sudden there was this horror-stricken look on my face. I started mumbling. Literally mumbling. I was thirty-nine years old; so I should have been an adult and able to say something intelligible. Wrong.

"It was unbelievable because I started saying words that weren't part of a sentence. I'd say, 'And Elvis, when he was young . . . he was young.' Everyone in the studio was keeled over from laughing. You could hear them just cracking up. My co-anchor at the time, Norma Rashid, found this especially humorous. Pat Barry, the weather guy, also found my flubber hilariously funny. All I could do to get myself out of this mess was to throw it back to Norma, which I did.

"Whenever there was a lot of tension in the newsroom, I would play a game with the news staff called 'Money Time.' Out of nowhere, I would suddenly jump up on the news desk, take whatever money was in my pocket, and toss it in the air, while

Norma Rashid and me. The team Cincinnati got its news from.

yelling, 'It's Money Time!' It really loosened everybody up when I did this and watching the entire newsroom scramble for dollars always provided much-needed comic relief. Everybody was laughing; but I always noticed that when the joke was over, less money was being returned to my wallet than I had initially tossed out. That speaks to either the integrity of journalists or to the fact that they're grossly underpaid.

"One of my other favorite stories from those days is about Santa Claus. It was Christmas Eve. So, like a lot of news stations, we thought we were going to be cute and open the news with a report on Santa's whereabouts. Norma was on vacation, so

I was there with Toria Tolley, who is now one of the anchors on *CNN Headline News* in Atlanta. We decided our lead story would be a report from the airport where the radar guy would spot something in the sky and, of course, it would be Santa Claus and his reindeer.

"So I opened the newscast as follows: 'Good evening. An unidentified flying object has been spotted over the greater Cincinnati airport. Let's go to Bob Jones at radar control.' I turned around and there was that big screen with an elderly guy named Bob Jones, who obviously had never been on television before, standing next to a radar screen. The crew had given him an earpiece so that he could hear me, but apparently it wasn't working. He was standing there, just staring into this camera with this big earpiece sticking out from his head, not saying a word. Not realizing he couldn't hear me, I turned to him and

Whenever things got dull on the set of the news, I would stand up and scream, "It's Money Time," and throw whatever money was in my wallet onto the studio floor. Deadline or not, the "journalists" would scramble for it.

once again said, 'Now let's go to the airport and check in with Bob Jones. Bob, what can you tell us?' The thing still wasn't working, so Bob was just standing there. So I'm going, 'Bob? Yo, Bob.' No Bob.

"Of course, the crew now realized what was going on, and they started losing it. Understand what I'd now done. I went live on the air and told all of Cincinnati that an unidentified flying object had been detected on a radar screen. No one yet knew that this was a joke. There'd been nothing about Good evening, Merry Christmas. I'd done this very seriously so that it would work. I certainly could never have turned back around to the camera and said, 'We're just kidding around, there's no Santa Claus, either.' So I was staring at the radar screen, praying for Bob to hear me. All I could hear was the cameraman yelling at Bob to talk to me.

"Finally he responded, and it was horrible. He started pointing at the radar screen, but having never been on television, he didn't know that you have to stand to the side so the camera can see the radar screen. So all you could see was his back, and he was standing there completely blocking our view of the screen. All I wanted him to say was, 'There's a sleigh, and it looks like I see some reindeer,' but we never got there with old Bob.

"Finally, I said, 'Yo, Bob. Does it look like a sleigh?' Now everybody was dying. I was biting my lip, trying not to laugh, because I knew at some point I had to turn around and look back into the camera. So finally I was losing it, and all I could say was, 'Bob, I guess what you're saying is the UFO looks like a reindeer and a sleigh. It's best for the kids to get to bed early, is that it?'

"Well, he never heard me say that, so we just cut him off. As I turn back around toward the camera, I've bitten my lip so hard in an effort not to laugh that I was actually bleeding. There's blood running down my chin. I had now told Cincinnati that there was an unidentified flying object and I had a bloody lip! Tears were streaming down my cheeks, and Pat Barry was in the background just going crazy from laughing; and everyone walked off the set because they were laughing so hard. And I was now supposed to go into my next story.

"The floor director saw that there was blood coming down my chin, so he started pointing at me, telling me to wipe my chin. I didn't realize what he was doing until I reached for my chin and saw blood. All I could say was, 'Oh, shit. Oh, my God, we'll be right back,' and cut to a commercial.

Why anyone ever watched our news was beyond me.

"Another valuable lesson I learned while anchoring the news was never to forget that you're wearing a microphone. One evening, after I had finished doing our early news, I was stand- ing around our studio getting ready to go to dinner. The *Newlywed Game* was now on. About four minutes into that show, we got a bulletin down in the newsroom—American planes were bombing Libya. All of a sudden Tom Kuelbs, our news director, came charging into my office, saying, 'Jerry, get up to the cam- era. We have to do a cut-in. We're at war with Libya. Toss it to Tom Brokaw in New York.'

"So I quickly stuck in my earpiece, set up the mike, and they turned on the camera down in the newsroom. I went on live and reported the following: 'We interrupt this program for this special bulletin. NBC is reporting that American planes have been spotted over Libya. And now, for more on that, we go to Tom Brokaw in New York.' And as I turned to the side, expect- ing to hook up with New York, the camera stayed on me. It was one of those very uncomfortable moments.

In position for another commentary.

"Again I repeated, 'We now go to Tom Brokaw in New York.' And the camera just kept staying on me. And I realized they didn't have the connection yet, so I went back on. I said, 'As I said, we have this report that apparently American planes have fired missiles at Libyan forces. Whether or not this is a final showdown with Khadafi, we don't know.' I'm just trying to fill the airtime. Finally, I get the signal. 'Okay now, we apparently have our feed. Let's go now to Tom Brokaw.' Still no Brokaw and then all of a sudden, boom, we're back to the *Newlywed Game*. Here I had just gone on the air to tell everyone we're at war, and suddenly I get cut off.

"So I took off my earpiece and walked off, saying, 'Thanks

for making me look like a real asshole.' And I walked out. What I didn't know was they hadn't yet shut off my microphone and put on the sound of the *Newlywed Game.* So even though you were looking at the *Newlywed Game,* you could hear me saying, 'Thanks for making me look like a real asshole.'

"Well, the phones at the station lit up. Nobody cared that we were at war; they were pissed that I had said 'asshole' on television. And the place went crazy. So then the news director heard this and came barreling into the newsroom, screaming, 'What the fuck's going on here? Jerry's mike is still on.'

"Well, guess what? That statement was heard by all of Cincinnati, too! The end of this story was that missiles were fired, but I was not. Since the news director was cursing as well, it was hard to single me out.

"When I decided to take on a special report, I jumped in with both feet. Night after night on the news, I would report on incidents without having any sort of emotion tied in. That was my job as an anchor—to stay neutral. But every now and then it was hard to stay neutral. The ever-expanding dilemma of the homeless was one such issue. It tugged at my heartstrings; but eventually I realized that I didn't really know what a homeless man or woman faced out on the streets. Perhaps I had to go through it myself—and that's exactly what I did. I decided to do a special five-part series called 'When the Streets Are Home,' where I would live as a homeless man for one week on the streets of Cincinnati. I wore a disguise, a beard, a mustache, and a wig, so that no one would recognize me. I was given three dollars and off I went to discover the horrors of street life.

"It didn't take me long to start panhandling. Three dollars doesn't go very far. I seemed to be hungrier than usual, too. Food suddenly became very important, as well as scarce. My first night out on the streets I found a park bench to sleep on, but I did something rather civilized—albeit idiotic for a homeless man. I took off my shoes and placed them at the end of the bench as if I was climbing into my comfortable king-sized bed at home. The cops came in the middle of the night to move me along, and it's funny when I think about it because they should have known I was a fish out of water, but they didn't.

"The streets were rough, but I found that the worst place I slept that week was in the homeless shelter for men. The smell was unbearable, and the overcrowding was out of control. I only made it one night in the shelter. Frankly, I found the street more appealing. I would nap in the public library, search for food in Dumpsters, and try to bathe in public restrooms.

"I remember one of my last nights on the street, I called my wife, Micki, and asked her to come meet me at a McDonald's. She brought our daughter, Katie, who was quite young at the time. The visit was scary for Katie because, although she recognized my voice, physically I was a total stranger to her. I'll never forget sitting in that restaurant, hoping no one would figure out that it was me; not because I was ashamed of what I was doing, but because I didn't want to blow my cover before I had the story done.

"Obviously, one week out on the streets didn't tell me what it felt like to be homeless. Even though I was uncomfortable, I always knew it would soon end and I'd be back to comfy living. I didn't suffer. But it did give me a chance to talk and visit with homeless people, who never would have talked to me if they'd known who I was.

"I learned some things from that experience. I learned that homelessness can happen to anyone. There's no one profile of a person likely to be out on the streets. Some come from good jobs and once stable families. For various reasons, their lives just fell apart. Of course, some are on the streets because state mental institutions have been shut down. Some are unemployable. Many are drunk a lot of the time. The truth is, facing such despair, it's not hard to see why they might want to drink. It's their only escape.

"Whatever the viewer learned from my reports, I know I certainly learned a lot. Indeed, doing the news was incredible for many reasons, but that series on the homeless would be my last special investigation as a newsman. Six weeks later *"The Jerry Springer Show"* would be born, and so would the next phase of my career."

"Okay, what a story . . . and, as promised, Jerry, when we return I'll give you my Final Thought."

SIX
God's Final Thought

"Jerry, amidst the bright lights of your television show, you continue to walk in the valley of the shadow of darkness. But I think there's still hope for you. Surely, you've made mistakes along the way. And though I would sooner smite the world with a swarm of locusts than give it another *Jerry Springer*, I'm going to send you back for a while. You're still an unfinished work.

"Keep fighting the good fight, against those who would suppress freedom—the elitist and arrogant of my flock—but try to stay out of trouble. You do seem a magnet for it. And remember, eventually you'll be back here. My talk show never gets cancelled.

"Go forth, Ringmaster, your circus is waiting."

Maybe Giuliani wouldn't be so bad. . . .

Suddenly, I awaken from my dream, a little drool on the pillow and the sleep still in my eyes. I'm completely uncertain of what has happened, but I feel well rested and alert. I get out of bed and do my usual morning routine. I'm in Los Angeles, the city of angels, shooting my movie. I call down to the kitchen of my hotel and order up room service—the usual: bran cereal, a bagel, coffee, and juice. A few minutes later, as always, there's a knock at the door—my breakfast. I sign the check and notice the newspaper sitting atop the silver tray.

I'm still uncertain about my dream. What did it all mean? Surely it's a message of some kind—but what? I turn on CNN, but keep the sound off. I'm feeling a bit reflective this morning. I open the paper and I see a one-inch column that says CNN and *Time* magazine have admitted that they failed to fact check a story about nerve gas usage during the Vietnam War. Their major, much-promoted stories were apparently not true. This admission came from two of the most respected news organizations in the world. I remember when this story broke, which made huge headlines. I think to myself, *How can the retraction be so small? This is the real story. . . .*

And they think my show is fake?

Whatever, I think I'll go over my script—

SEVEN
A Show Is Born

I met Burt Dubrow in Cincinnati while I was still a news anchor on WLWT. He was producing a regionally syndicated show called *Braun & Company* for Multimedia, the company that owned our station. Occasionally, Burt would ask me to come on his show and tell jokes and improvise stories and just have some fun. It was a really loose atmosphere, and you just never knew what would happen. But my bosses felt that these appearances weren't great for my image as their news anchor. So eventually they asked me to stop. And I totally understood. How could I possibly be dancing with the Chippendales one minute and reporting on the Gulf War the next?

By 1991, Multimedia owned, not only the station on which I was doing the news, but also the *Phil Donahue Show*, *Sally Jessy Raphael*, and *Rush Limbaugh*. At the time, these were among the three most popular talk shows in the country. The company was looking to add another to their list—perhaps a successor to *Donahue*, who was nearing retirement. Burt had already successfully launched the *Sally Jessy Raphael Show* so he knew how to get a new talk show off the ground. My appearances on *Braun & Company* were pretty popular in Cincinnati; and maybe because of that, or for whatever reason, Burt, unbeknownst to me, suggested me for the job of host. Walter Bartlett, then the CEO of Multimedia, who was also responsible for

In addition to hosting duties, I was also the official food-taster for Universal. Here I am making sure this cake is safe for Sally Jessy Raphael and then-chairman Greg Meidel.

WLWT, was reluctant to give the go-ahead. He didn't want to lose me as anchor. Our ratings put us at number one in the market, and no reasonable news department would give up their main anchor just so he could do a fluff talk show.

Burt was afraid to say anything to me for a while because he wasn't sure how Walter was going to respond. Walter still had reservations. As I said, he didn't want me to stop anchoring the news. If we went ahead with this new show, it would have to be in *addition* to the news. Well, finally Walter said yes. He took me to lunch and told me. We agreed that we would shoot the show in Cincinnati, so I could still do both jobs. I'd tape the show in the morning, and do the news at 5:30, 6:00, and 11:00 P.M. It was a long, long day.

It's strange when I look back on this today, but they never even auditioned me for the host job; I was simply assigned to the task. I often tell people that if I had auditioned, I'm absolutely certain I would never have been given the job. Let's face it, I have a face for radio and a voice for newspapers. . . .

And so, in September 1991, *"The Jerry Springer Show"* was born, sort of.

The original idea was to do important and serious topical interviews with politicians, celebrities, and other prominent people. Shows about the Waco, Texas, massacre, runaway teens who live on the street, teenage junkies, and school prayer filled the first season roster of shows. We also wanted to do what we called "feel good" shows. We did makeover shows, hypnotism, and even played "the Newlywed Game!" Sally Jessy Raphael, Oliver North, Richard Simmons, and Jesse Jackson were all guests my first year. Needless to say, we've come a long way from those days. Surely they'd never agree to be guests on my show today.

We started off with what I'll refer to as a very light staff of 9 people headed by Terry Murphy—truly a miracle worker. To give you some idea of what that means, today I have a staff of over 80 producing the same number of shows a year. This original production team was incredible because everyone had to wear as many hats as they could fit on their head. There wasn't any room for ego, and amazingly enough, they pulled it off.

The concept of re-creating *Donahue* screamed from every nook and cranny. Our set, which was almost identical to Donahue's, as well as my questions, the setup, and the interview style were all purposely directed toward that goal. My suits, my "big boy" haircut, even my glasses were all intended to replicate the "Donahue" image.

Our first show was a family reunion. We reunited a mother, named Jane, with her two children, whom she hadn't seen in 35 years. A Georgia court had ordered her children to be taken away from her in 1956 as she lay hospitalized after being brutally shot several times by her first husband, who subsequently shot and killed himself. Since she had no income, the court took her children away from her. Jane sobbed uncontrollably onstage as she shared her sad story. Suddenly, from the audience, a young man stood up and asked Jane if she would recognize her son if she saw him today. And before she could even answer, he shouted, "Hi, Mom!" and ran up to the stage to embrace his long-lost mother. Jane was also reunited with her daughter, Sandy, as well as her four grandchildren.

There was lots of hugging and kissing, bouquets of flowers for everyone, and even tears of joy. It was a very emotional reunion that seemed, at the time, to be a heartfelt and sincere reconnection.

Now, even though we started out as a straight, traditional

On our first show we brought long-lost loved ones together.
Years later those flowers would have been used as a weapon.

In a very early show (with a very early haircut) I sat down for a one-on-one interview with Jesse Jackson.

talk show in the Donahue-Oprah mold, few thought I had much of a future.

John Kiesewetter, the television critic for the *Cincinnati Enquirer,* has chronicled my career in television in greater detail than anyone else. He has been appropriately tough on me over

the years, but always fair. It was John, in reviewing my first episode of *"The Jerry Springer Show,"* who advised me not to "give up my desk job anchoring the news."

It was difficult in the beginning juggling my role as talk show host by day and serious newsman by night. My bosses at

Multimedia feared the talk show would tarnish my image as a broadcast journalist. And they had a point. In Kiesewetter's words: "The daytime Springer can't be seen as the lovable liberal leader we know here in Cincinnati because that act simply won't play in Los Angeles, Dallas, or any other big city. The daytime Springer must be a clone of Sally, Oprah, and Phil. We accepted him as a TV commentator because we recognized his passion for truth, justice, and the American way, even if we didn't agree with his opinions."

But for me the talk show became an extension of my beliefs in all of those things. My first day on the job as a talk show host gave me the same rush I'd felt the day I was sworn in as mayor or the day I did my first commentary or newscast. And after we taped our first show, I felt a kind of freedom I had never felt before in any of those previous positions. It was an emotional emancipation I hadn't ever been able to display as a calculating councilman or sedentary anchorman. Although some might say that I'd probably crossed that line more than most other anchors.

Our early *Springer* shows were sort of a mixed bag, trying new and different ideas to help better define who we were and who we wanted to be. One thing became very clear early on though; we were never going to be the "next" Donahue. We were becoming the first Jerry Springer!

Whenever we would do a show that I was personally excited by, like an interview with Oliver North or Jesse Jackson, our ratings would slip in the overnight tally. Because of my political background, politically themed shows were always my favorite in the early days. But even if I liked that kind of talk show—no one else did. I could tap into my own experiences for these interviews and even my intellect a little (what little I have).

The show continued on, even though our ratings were barely

calculable. We were only in a few of the major markets—some nineteen cities in all by the end of our first season. We all knew that if the show was going to be a success, it would have to be seen in more markets. Tom Shannon was our head sales manager at the time, and with incredible spirit, and a lot of blue smoke and mirrors, he made it his job to hawk our rather nondescript show. The time had come to syndicate. The economics for a regional show just weren't there. Tom met with Judy Gerrard, who at the time was running the NBC O&Os (stations owned and operated by the network, as opposed to being owned privately).

Burt and Tom took Judy to dinner in Cincinnati, where I was introduced to her for the first time. The following day she came to a taping of the show, and according to Burt, she loved what she saw. That opened the door for Tom to make a deal with Judy to air our shows on their stations. But there was one caveat to that deal—we had to shoot out of the WMAQ station in Chicago! Oh, and by the way, I would still remain as the anchor at WLWT, doing the same three evening news reports and commentaries from my desk in Cincinnati. Burt suggested to my management (and to me) that I would be able to handle the commute and that I would be "available no less than four nights a week." This concept meant that I would be living in airports and on interstates, and yet I knew that if we were going to succeed, I had to do it.

I also knew the move would accomplish many things for us. One of the biggest would be our ability to book better and more famous guests. It also put us in more markets. We would now be seen in New York, Chicago, Philadelphia, San Francisco, Boston, Detroit, Washington, and Miami. I would fly to Chicago every day, tape the show, and return to Cincinnati in the afternoon to do the evening news. Burt got very excited by the possibilities of the move; and at the time it never dawned on me that this "commuting" would take a toll on me, physically or mentally.

So in only our second season, we embarked on a journey that would ultimately become *"The Jerry Springer Show"* of today, though no one would have or could have known it at the time.

Without a doubt, Burt Dubrow is an executive producer with great vision. He ignited the flame that years later, depending on your point of view, is either burning society—or shedding some light on it. And Multimedia was very good at what they were building, slowly rolling out the show and penetrating the major markets one by one. My bosses at Multimedia allowed us to develop and grow with a lot of autonomy, which was important to the growth of the show. My producers were able to push the

This was the first show we did in Chicago. You could say these guests "christened" our stage. We've changed the carpet since then.

envelope creatively, putting out some of the freshest and most memorable moments in talk.

Terry Murphy, our first senior producer, and really the person who was most hands-on with our show, took over as executive producer as Burt started relinquishing the reins little by little those first few seasons. She set us on a course that would carve out our little place in television history. The battles she had to endure every day would make a book in itself. I'm grateful for what she did.

Of course, today we follow a formula that has taken us in new directions. Richard Dominick, currently my executive producer, is, more than anyone else, responsible for taking our show to the outer edge and, in the process, making this the number-one talk show in America. If you were casting him in a movie, you'd have Robert DeNiro play him, or Joe Pesci, in

That's Terry Murphy, Steve Hyrniewicz, and Annette Grundy lounging around the set after a day's adventure.

Goodfellas. Richard doesn't belong to the Mafia—never did—but he doesn't mind having you wonder. He's often reading books about the mob—puffing endlessly on his impressive supply of cigars—evoking a persona of toughness that, in truth, masks loyalty, a heart of gold, and a wealth of creativity. He's a dear friend and a great partner.

Richard came on board as a favor to us while we were still shooting out of Cincinnati. He was asked if he wanted to work on the show, and he originally had said, "No!" Then we asked if he would consider coming onboard for two weeks. He agreed . . . and seven years later he's now the self-described "devil on my shoulder."

Richard describes the first time he met me like this:

Richard Dominick,

PRODUCER/CURRENT EXECUTIVE PRODUCER 1991–PRESENT

Jerry walks into my office in his street clothes . . . jeans and an untucked rumpled shirt. He had a sweater on over the shirt and his collar was all messed up . . . not too unlike the way he dresses today! His hair was all over the place, but he had a Kennedyesque-meets-Woody-Allen kind of quality about him. This was my very first day on the job, and I remember seeing him a short time later and there was this totally different man standing there. He had slicked-back hair that looked like "Big Boy" and he was wearing a banker's suit. We called him "Perry Jerry Mason" in those days. He looked like this man in a box. All of those casual qualities were gone. He wasn't Woody Allen or Kennedyesque anymore, he was just this uncomfortable guy in

This picture was taken moments before Richard Dominick and Annette Grundy kicked my butt out. Richard and Annette handle the stress of the show very well. I, by contrast, occasionally lose it.

a bad banker's suit! I wanted to loosen him up a little, but the image they were going for at the time was of this stiff guy.

Richard had worked with a bright young producer, Annette Grundy, prior to joining our staff and suggested we hire her. She came onboard about three weeks after his arrival and stayed with our show until the 1997/1998 season. She was one of our best producers over the years. Of course, she remembers a little different story about meeting me for the first time:

Annette Grundy,
PRODUCER/SR. PRODUCER 1991–1997

It was my first day on the job and I went to the hair and makeup room to introduce myself to Jerry. As I met him, I realized he was standing there in his boxer shorts, which were white with red hearts on them. You had to admire someone who felt comfortable enough around people and realized that you had a job to do and he had a job to do, and that's what made it work. I had to brief him for the show and he needed to get dressed. It was never insulting or lewd. It was like being around family. But the red hearts always stuck with me! In fact, I always looked forward to seeing him to see what cute underwear he was wearing.

I never realized that the clothes I wore left such an impression on my coworkers. Hey, I'm just a guy, and really, at 54 I figure I can make my own decision about what to wear. And how I look. Wrong. After my first show aired, Mary Beth Crocker, who wrote the style section for the *Cincinnati Enquirer*, did an entire column on my "new TV look." She said that my "revamped style was a long way from the staid dark suits and erratic haircuts Cincinnatians have seen over the previous decade." She even reported that I would be getting my hair "shaped" every Monday. (It was becoming clear to me that nothing about my life would be private anymore.)

But despite my loud demonstrations against the oncoming wave of wardrobe change, people have been trying to upgrade my image over the years. My former personal assistant, Tracy Douglass, took it upon herself to dress me "just right." My wardrobe in the early days used to make her crazy.

Tracy Douglass,
PERSONAL ASSISTANT 1994–1998

Jerry's the easiest guy in the world to shop for. His uniform for the show is a Giorgio Armani suit, a white shirt, and a colored tie. Every new season I would go to Armani and ask what new dark suits they had for Jerry. They inevitably would say, "The same ones we had last season, Tracy. We have black, navy, and gray." So each year I would pick out five or six new suits for Jerry, some new white shirts, and a couple of new ties. It was that simple.

We used to have these little battles over keeping Jerry looking hip when he made appearances outside of his own show. We never had a real argument ever, but I definitely tried to get him out of his uniform of Slim Fit Jeans and nappy balled-up sweaters, white tube socks, and black shoes! At least I got him out of his plaid shirts and pilling sweaters.

Sheila Rosenbaum, Betsy Bergman, and Tracy Douglass.

Betsy Bergman and I would pull our hair out because we just couldn't break Jerry of his uniform. *TV Guide* had done a story where they rated all of the talk show hosts on the air based on their wardrobe. *TV Guide* would give them little microphones instead of stars as the rating scale, and Jerry got half a microphone for his rating out of a possible four! In fact, as his "wardrobe consultant," I felt like a real idiot because Jerry would go out on *Letterman* looking like such a geek! I would get a call from Richard Dominick asking me what I was thinking, and I would have to explain to him that I had bought the right outfit for Jerry to wear, but he wore what he wanted anyway! In fact, he made me leave his room once because I was insisting he wear a different outfit for a Conan O'Brien appearance. He said, as a 52-year-old man, he wasn't going to be told what to wear!

Another thing that Jerry hates is having to wear makeup for television. He hates having to sit and have his makeup done. He'd come back from a weekend away and he'd have a little tan,

**and he thought it would be fine to go on the air looking that way.
Well, as anyone who has ever seen someone on television without makeup can tell you, those lights can be harsh and unflatter-
ing. But Jerry just doesn't care! If he could get away with it, he'd
go on the air in whatever clothes he came in wearing that day,
scruffy hair, and no makeup. I don't think you'll ever see Jerry
on *People* magazine's "Best Dressed List!"**

Ouch . . . but I suppose it's true. I have gotten a little better
though, and all with Tracy's cajoling!

In 1993 I finally announced that I would be leaving WLWT
after ten years to devote all of my efforts toward building the
success of *"The Jerry Springer Show,"* which was now demanding my full time in Chicago, though my home was still
Cincinnati. Frankly, it was inevitable. My final newscast was on
January 22, 1993. An interesting side note is that my replacement was to be former mayor and congressman Charlie Luken.
Had I started a trend in Cincinnati for job placement after serving as mayor?

Anyway, my national ratings on *"The Jerry Springer Show"*
were strong enough to encourage many of the stations running
the show to renew with us for one to two more seasons, and I felt
it was only fair to devote my attention to keeping our show a success. I believe that my absence toward the end of my run at
WLWT was detrimental to their broadcast. I believe it confused
the viewer to only see me three or so days a week, and I was
becoming more known as a talk show host than a news guy.
James A. Clayton, who was my station manager when I left
WLWT, agreed with me. He felt it sent a mixed message to the
viewers to see me interviewing nudists in the afternoon and then
reading serious news at night. And he was right.

My last night on the air at WLWT was a tough one. Cincinnati had been my home for 25 years. And though I would face my viewers—fans and critics—many times over the following years, I was touched by a particular story by John Kiesewetter that ran in the *Cincinnati Enquirer* on the eve of my final broadcast.

For 2 1/2 minutes time stood still every night in my house. When Jerry Springer read his commentary, I listened to every word. I didn't always agree with the loveable liberal. But his eloquent essays, sometimes bordering on the poetic, made Channel Five's newscast number 1 from 1987 to '92. He made me think, laugh, cry, or scream in anger at the TV. He stimulated my mind, a destination seldom reached by the typical TV anchor. His nightly commentary was live TV at its raw, powerful best. Exciting and unpredictable. He told me the news, then told me his views. . . .

Whether I agreed with him or not, often his words—a twist of a phrase, a summary zinger—would leave me in awe of his writing skill, privately wishing I'd said that.

As the *Springer Show* continued to forge ahead, my critics began to grow—in staggering numbers. To this day I offer no excuses or apologies for what we do. Acting as "the Ringmaster" is what I do for a living. It's my job. It hasn't affected my passion for politics, changed my opinion on my religious beliefs, or my overall view on life.

My producers, with the extraordinary vision and leadership of Richard Dominick, had carved out a formula that was creating ratings—big ratings. In 1995 we were consistently beating Jay Leno and David Letterman in the Los Angeles market. We

This woman was defending her right to work as a stripper. A fight broke out, but she held her own.

were on the heels of Oprah and Sally Jessy. It's a pretty simple explanation really.

We took notice that if we followed in the footsteps of our competition, doing a straight talk show, so to speak, it would inevitably lead us straight to lower ratings. It was time to listen to the public, to show another side of life rarely, if ever, seen on television. It was rougher, but real—and certainly wilder—but viewers loved it, in overwhelming numbers. Of course, along with the increasing popularity came the critics. It didn't and doesn't matter. People want to be entertained when they watch television, particularly daytime television. Look at the long-term success of soap operas.

Television has to be entertaining and interesting in order to succeed. No one ever said that every show has to be *important* or *informational*. My show isn't a platform for me, it's a platform for my guests; and in the spirit of the First Amendment, they have every right to that platform. But there's a collective voice out there that would like you to believe otherwise.

> It's really a First Amendment issue. As debasing and violent as "The Jerry Springer Show" has become, media critics and politicians, such as Sen. Joe Lieberman or William Bennett, shouldn't have the power to silence him.
>
> —PHIL DONAHUE
> TALK SHOW HOST

I believe the year was 1989. William Bennett had come to Cincinnati to address a large group of business types. I think it was the Chamber of Commerce. It was a packed house, and he told the audience, in a momentary aside, how impressed he was with the commentary he had heard the night before by a local news anchor. It was something relating to values, and he wished everyone had had a chance to hear it.

If today he remembers that incident, he would probably be gagging, for the person whose ideas he was so openly praising happened to have been me, delivering my nightly commentary.

Now, beyond the obvious irony of William Bennett, now the chief critic of my show, having such nice words to say about me, is the reality that there is much of what Bennett espouses that I find very attractive—and have no difficulty agreeing with.

Let's face it. It's hard to argue against his point that the world would be a better place if everyone were virtuous. And though he does come across as being annoyingly self-righteous, often posturing himself as America's police chief of virtue, he does give good speeches and his books on morality are well worth reading.

In truth, he can be quite engaging. But there are problems—and the point of contention is not what you might expect. Look, I totally understand how our show isn't for everyone. In fact, I've often said that I don't watch it myself; but I think Bennett runs into dangerous territory when he enlists the power or influence of the government into either censoring the show or trying to shut it down altogether.

Now obviously that's not going to happen. Indeed, the more he attacks and protests, the more popular the show becomes. In fact, he's the one who pushed us to number one. But let's face it, the notion that certain powers can control or limit what other people can watch, say, or believe is pretty scary in a free society.

Please understand. It is not important that anyone approve of this show. In fact, it's perfectly okay to actually hate it and to never watch it. But if the idea "America" is to mean anything, it is critical that we protect the show.

Why?

Well, only if expression outside the mainstream is protected are the rest of us protected. What do I mean by that?

Look.

The First Amendment isn't there for *Time* magazine or *Newsweek* or *The New York Times*. Those publications don't need it. They reflect the majority mainstream point of view anyway, so what protection do they need? We, the majority, are already on their side.

It's the expressions, written, spoken, and broadcast on the edges—those words, ideas, and lifestyles that don't reflect the majority thinking, that are alien to it, even offensive—that's what we have to protect. Because only when these edges are safe are the rest of us in the middle safe as well.

You see, let's say a show like ours, or Howard Stern's, or Rush Limbaugh's were pressured off the air. The lesson would then be that you would only be free to say what you want if what you said was acceptable to the mainstream powers. Suddenly, none of us would really be free then. We'd all have to worry that what we said or expressed was approved by the government or the authorities because otherwise the airwaves would be closed to us.

So I might not like what certain guests say on our show; I might not like their manners, or their lifestyles, or their politics. I certainly can't stand what the neo-Nazis or the Klan espouse; but I would fight, and fight hard, to see that the guests on my show have as much right to be on television as anyone else in our country.

William Bennett doesn't get it—or would prefer not to get it. It's easier to call people trash than to honor the principle of free speech and expression and to trust the concept of freedom, which implies that everyone has a right to be heard—and the most horrible ideas will ultimately fall of their own weight.

I'd love to debate him in person on this issue; but every time we're invited to appear together—be it Larry King or some other national news program—he declines. He can't lose a debate if he's not there. And I'd even agree that the chairs would be nailed down so that things wouldn't get out of hand. The truth is, I'd enjoy the opportunity. I'd probably learn something. And if he'd listen up for a moment, maybe he would too.

When I left television news, many of my one-time supporters, either from the world of politics and/or the world of news, saw my departure as selling out. The truth is, I haven't changed a bit. I'm as liberal as I've always been, and I have no trouble sleeping at night. I work in show business, and like the name infers, it's a business—like any other. My job is to entertain. But my close friend Jene Galvin often reminds me that my audience hasn't changed a bit over the years. From politics, to news, to talk show host, my constituency has always been the same—the young, the working class, minorities, liberals, populists, and the college educated. I've always felt a real next-door neighbor, best buddy, or "one of the guys" connection with the public. Maybe that's why its always been "Jerry" instead of Mr. Springer, or Mr. Mayor, or Councilman. It's been that way for over thirty years.

Now even admitting that our show can be really silly and stupid at times, I work real hard at it. You see, this is a competitive business; and if I'm going to stay in the game, I have to work harder than anybody else because I'm not good-looking

Me and the boys. That's right, everyone on this stage is a man. One of them is extremely uncomfortable.

enough or that great of a talent that people will keep watching our show if we go soft. It's really no different from when I ran for political office. Whatever you're doing, be the best you can be at it. When I'm not taping the six shows a week that we do, I'm usually off promoting the heck out of *"The Jerry Springer Show."* In politics, we called that campaigning. I have been nothing if not consistent and honest about our show from the beginning. It is the silliest, craziest, most outrageous show around. But . . . if you don't like what you see in the mirror, don't break the mirror; change the reflection . . . or the channel.

Have I sold out? Not at all. I'm still as liberal as I've ever been and work hard on those causes. The point is, I've enjoyed every job I've ever had. I loved doing the news and being in political office. Every time I have moved on to something else, there's always been some public reaction on why I supposedly "can't" or "should not." When I went from mayor to doing news, they said to me, "You can't do the news; you're a politician." Then when I became an anchor and a commentator, everyone thought, *He's too opinionated.* And with my talk show, it was, *What does he know about being an entertainer?*

Look. I just want to go to work like anyone else and do the best that I can. I'll admit, I often feel that my life has been one lucky break after another. For that I thank God every day. It really is wonderful that I get to meet the most interesting people—and I never run out of things to say at a dinner party.

> **We are a Jerry Springer World.**
>
> —BILL MAHER
> HOST, <u>POLITICALLY INCORRECT</u>

EIGHT
Behind the Scenes

Producing a television show is like any other business that depends on an assembly line setup. Everyone has his or her job to do, and if someone or something falls short anywhere along the way, the show will suffer. We shoot two hundred new shows each and every year. We primarily shoot Monday to Wednesday, taping two shows a day.

An episode of *"The Jerry Springer Show"* begins with you, the viewer. We have taken great strides to ensure that you are seeing the type of programming that appeals to a mass audience, despite the protest of our critics.

One of the most frequently asked questions I get is, "How do you find your guests?" Oddly enough, we usually don't; they find us. There is only one way to get on *"The Jerry Springer Show"* . . . and that is if you **want** to be on. It all starts off with the tease questions that run on every episode. You know, the ones that come on as we go into or out of a commercial break:

"Do you or does somebody you know live a bizarre or unusual lifestyle?"

"Do you have a secret?"

"Are you having an affair?"

and the most popular one . . .

"Do you need a paternity test?"

Form 1 (top):

SHOW "Mistresses Attack"
BOX 403
PAGE 3
DAY Tuesday
DATE 5/5
NAME Paul

CART 1 Are you in a "A" + think...
CART 2 Did you have a 1 night stand would you...
CART 3 Are you torn between 2 lovers + want to end it w/ 1 of them
TYPE General

initial	cart	name	phone	message
	M	DANA		thinks ex-husband is gay + she slept w/his best friend
	M	RYAN		wants to get back together w/ ex-love
	M	Mike		he's a super sex freak who likes anal sex + other wierd stuff
	M	FRED		wants to sleep w/ friend's wife (?)
		John		call after 4pm he's a drug addict + an alcoholic + wants to be on show
				Do show about sickle cell anemia
				He's a real man who wants to confront abusive husbands on show
				it's a real man who wants to confront transvestites on show (?)

Form 2 (bottom):

SHOW IT "Mistresses Attack"
BOX 403
PAGE 2
DAY Tuesday
DATE 5/5
NAME Paul

CART 1 Are you in a "A" + think its time to make a decision PROD. JB
CART 2 Did you have a 1 night stand would you like to confront person PROD.2 JW
CART 3 Are you torn between 2 lovers + want to end it w/ 1 of them PROD.3 MC
TYPE General

initial	cart	name	phone	message
	M	DA NESHA		wants to confront her slut friend "RACHAEL" who lies about being black
		MARLENE		Do A Father's Day show
		BLACK SHADOW		He is in the ZULU Crew / wants to confront rival group
P	T	TIZZER (?)		Do show about Bi sexual people who get it on w/ ANIMALS
P	T	Ashley		? (sounded drunk)
		Female		?
	M	NIKKI		Do A sexy Mother + Daughter contest
		John		can not believe that Jerry exploits sin
T		Mary		says her family broke her + her boyfriend up
		Patrick		"Strippers, hookers, porn stars wants more + more + more"
T		LISA		Her BABY's father is dating her best friend
T		Dennis		get a Boxing Ring + have Jerry referee
T		BRIAN		Bestiality "rules"
T		AMBROSE		FIANCEE'S BABY has been taken by her parents wants to confront them (this is court mandated) – FATHER is a sex offender

These calls to action generate anywhere from 1000 to 3000 phone calls a day! If you've ever tried calling into our show, you get an automated answering machine that gives you several options. "Press one if you're really a man living as a woman, press two if you want to confront your husband's mistress . . . " And so on.

These calls get placed in what's called a "cart." Interns sort the carts by logging each and every phone call that comes in. They take down all of the information you leave, such as your name, your phone number, and the reason for your call. I'm amazed at the sheer volume of calls we receive, but even more incredible are some of the messages we get.

Once the calls are sorted, an associate producer can choose the potential guests on a first-come first-serve basis by initialing the ones he or she wants. Producers then call the people of interest and ask them some initial qualifying questions. They want to make absolutely sure that you're for real, that you aren't too "shy" to appear on television, and, of course, be certain that what you're saying is the truth.

Most of our producers have an area that he or she specializes in when it comes to the topics they produce. For example, one producer might handle all of our shows dealing with the Ku Klux Klan, while another producer deals mostly with transsexuals, lesbians, and three-way love affairs.

Once producers take their leads from the cart, it's up to them to follow up. Usually an associate producer will do a lot of the legwork. It's important to us that we can verify whether or not the story you are telling us is real. We will ask for all sorts of backup to authenticate your claims. Marriage certificates, wedding photos, paternity results, "conjugal" photos, and other family members to corroborate your story might all be requested. If you can't provide the proof, we can't put you on the air. It's that simple.

We don't pay guests to appear on our show, which is a question I'm often asked. Plain and simple, although some shows do, we don't, mostly because we don't have the budget for it, although we do pay for itemized expenses. But also we want our guests to be there because they *want* to be there, not for the few hundred bucks they might get somewhere else for making up a good story. If your story is outrageous, if you want to be on, and you're telling the truth, chances are you'll get on our show.

If we do go ahead with your story, we ask you to sign a waiver that says that if you are not telling us the truth, we can sue you. We even videotape this process to ensure it is the same person signing. And there have been a few people in the past that we have actually had to sue. Usually, when the producer explains that particular caveat to the guest, he or she gets a little scared and decides not to go through with the show. In the end, it saves all of us a lot of embarrassment.

That's not to say however that the wool hasn't been pulled over our eyes. I am sure that, like all talk shows on television, and even the news, there have been guests who have successfully appeared on our show and simply were not telling a true story. But out of 14,000-plus guests over seven years, the staff of "*The Jerry Springer Show*" has gone to great lengths to extinguish any show where we weren't "buying" the story. Chances aren't likely that a guest will actually make it to a taping if they are trying to pull a fast one over on us. The production staff asks for a lot of proof before they book a guest for a show. But sometimes, and it has happened, a guest will sneak through all the scrutiny and make it on the air.

All of that being said . . . there is a well-known story of a Canadian comedy group from Toronto who appeared on our show in February of 1995. They masqueraded themselves as an outrageous quartet. They represented themselves to be a real-life husband and wife, and a baby-sitter and her boyfriend. Their story wasn't an unusual one for our show, which involved the husband supposedly having an affair with the baby-sitter. A pretty typical, if not banal, story line for our show. It turns out, of course, that these four actors were, in fact, fake guests who'd made it through the system.

After the show aired, they went public, claiming that we fake our show. This public admission made headlines everywhere. Let it be known that, like any other guest who appears on our show, they were put through the same screening process, and provided what we felt was legitimate backup to verify their story. Having successfully done this on other talk shows, this group knew what to expect in terms of preinterviews, and they were well-rehearsed and prepared. Ultimately, these "actors" knew it was good publicity for them and would help bolster their notoriety as actors. But . . . we were not amused by their trickery and sued them for our expenses.

Recently, one of the tabloid shows ran a story claiming that they'd found 14 guests who had appeared on our show and were fake—that is, their stories were fake; the fights were staged and a producer was behind it all. These guests all signed releases swearing to us that their stories were true, so they were either lying to us or to the folks at the tabloid show. But I'm going to assume for the moment that they got it right—that these guests were, in fact, fake. On that point, they may have done a good job. But here's what's misleading about their report. The implication of this story, as picked up by some papers across the country, was that our show was fake—that we make all this up.

Well, we could, of course. We're not a news program; we're an entertainment show. We, like a soap opera or a sitcom, could script the whole thing if we chose to do so. But the truth is—we don't.

We don't because I want the show to be real. I think it's much more effective, entertaining, and compelling if the viewer is sitting at home watching and going, "Wow, these folks are real. It's amazing!" If it's fake, then we might as well do a soap opera where everyone's a good actor and they're all drop-dead gorgeous.

So simply put, our show is real. Now understand, since I started the show seven years ago, we've had over 14,000

STILL AIR VT-X #57 FRANK C-1 JOHN C-2

2 CHY AIR 1 SAFETY #56

Here's our war-room. I'm not sure what any of those buttons or switches do, but it sure is an impressive display.

guests—nearly sixty different producers. Surely, some of those guests—yes, even some of my producers, may have crossed the line, or been less than straightforward in following the rules. So here and there we've had a rogue producer, here and there a guest who's made up a story or seriously embellished on

it. So this tabloid show found 14 such guests. My guess is there're more. What if it's 25, 50, or even 100? That would mean that out of the 14,000 guests who have appeared on *"The Jerry Springer Show,"* 13,900 have been truthful. Where was that headline?

So again—it wouldn't matter if this stuff was all made up; but the fact is, it's not. It's real—overwhelmingly real.

The tabloid show chose to ignore that reality—and ran, instead, with the sexier implication of fakery. In fairness to them though, as a tabloid show, they're not held to the same standard as a legitimate news program.

But there is a little bit of hypocrisy here worthy of note. Do you ever notice how these tabloid shows—in fact, even the legitimate news programs—invariably blast our show during sweeps, running their special series attacking us during weeks when ratings are being measured? And in saying how awful the fights are they will always show clips of our fights in their promos and headlines—trying to attract viewers to their own program. If the fights are so horrible for television, why do they show them 20 times a day, promoting their own show? Hmm . . .

Our producers try to put together shows that have all of the essential elements and then some. That's why you'll always get other family members appearing in almost every show. We want to bring you, the viewing audience, the best and most entertaining show possible; so we leave no turn unstoned and no stone unturned. We *want* the whole kit and caboodle. That's what makes us different. If we don't show you all sides of a story, then we become like the rest of the media, purposely skewing your opinion in one direction.

Once a guest is selected to appear on our show, we will provide transportation to Chicago and pay for the hotel. That in itself is often a production. Nancy Kleinau is our staff travel coordinator. Without her hard work, many of our shows would never come together.

Nancy Kleinau,

SHOW TRAVEL AGENT 1995–PRESENT

I've had to transport some pretty interesting things since working at *"The Jerry Springer Show."* Once I had to get an 800-pound man to Chicago to do the show. The problem was that the man was from a small town in Ohio and the airport didn't have one of those carts that always beep in the airports when they are driving through, usually with elderly passengers. We really needed one of those because a man who weighs that much can't travel very far on foot.

So I had to get six baggage handlers to meet him curbside with a luggage cart to transport him to the plane. I had bought him two seats on Southwest, but he was given five, with two facing him, so he could put his legs up.

Another time I had to get Lori and Dori to the show. Nobody had told me that they were conjoined twins until about four hours before the flight, so originally I had them in seats that were not next to each other. Luckily, the airline made accommodations for them so they could travel "together." Clearly there was no other choice.

My job is not an easy one. I'm usually not dealing with rocket scientists. I once had one woman miss eight flights in a row! She kept on showing up at the wrong airport. Then she would show up at the wrong terminal. It can be very frustrating because I can have a whole show booked on their flights; and if one party backs out of the show, I have to cancel all the flights because we always have to have all parties in a story represented or there's no show. I probably have about 80 canceled tickets a month.

It's important for me to book the opposing parties on separate flights because we want the show to happen on the air, not in the air. I've had a couple of close calls because of guests missing their flights. I've learned to not book the flights close together because inevitably one party will miss their flight; and if they're on the same flight, all hell could break loose.

I do have an interesting relationship with the airlines. When I call up, I come up on the screen as "Nancy, The Jerry Springer Show." They tell me, "Oh, we can always tell your people a mile away." But I know that's not always the case because I got a call from a gate agent last year saying, "I'm standing here looking at a driver's license that says Ronald Smith and there's a woman in front of me." I said nonchalantly back to him, "Jerry Springer guest, transsexual." And that was all. He said, "Never mind." And let him on the plane.

I've seen anything and everything, and there's nothing, nothing that could faze me anymore . . . that is, until the guy called me about that horse.

We usually bring guests in the night before their taping, but sometimes it may be a few days early, depending on the complexity of the show and when it will tape.

The best kind of show—for us or, for that matter, any talk show—is when a surprise is sprung on one of the guests. If handled properly, it can be great. If not, it can be a disaster—as, of course, was the case with *The Jenny Jones Show.*

Briefly, what happened was that there was a guest appearing on a secret-crush show who was told that someone was about to come out who had a crush on him. It turned out that his secret admirer was, in fact, a guy. The guest, apparently humiliated by this circumstance—that his admirer was another man, not a

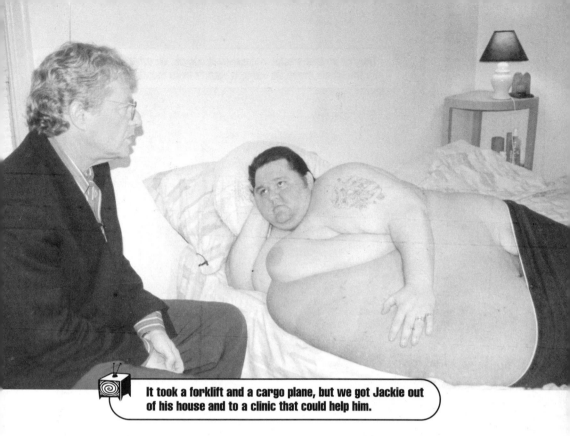

It took a forklift and a cargo plane, but we got Jackie out of his house and to a clinic that could help him.

woman, and not wanting a national television audience to conclude that he was gay—was so upset that two days later he killed his admirer. He was, of course, convicted, but *The Jenny Jones Show* received a lot of heat for creating this situation. Their defense had been that the guest knew—or, in fact, had been told—that his admirer might be a man and he hadn't objected to it, so they shouldn't be held responsible.

In fairness, we don't know what he was told, so it's not proper to offer judgment here. But in defense of Jenny Jones, this case tells us more about the state of homophobia in our society than it does about the state of *The Jenny Jones Show*.

Here's what I mean. Let's take the exact same situation. A male guest appears and he's about to be surprised by a secret admirer. But let's say that in this case the person who comes out

They're an interracial, homosexual couple. On other shows that would be the whole story. On ours, it wasn't even mentioned.

from behind the curtain is not another guy but, in fact, a woman, except that he doesn't think the woman is very attractive; he thinks she's downright homely looking. He's so humiliated that on national television, in his mind, an ugly woman professed her love to him, that two days later he kills her. There's not one person in America who would be blaming Jenny Jones. We'd all be saying, "How dare that pig of a man shoot a woman because he thought she was ugly."

No, it's just because in our society, we still think that a gay guy professing his love to another man is reason to be humiliated, so we start blaming Jenny Jones for the homicide. The disastrous consequences of that incident on *The Jenny Jones Show* tell us more about the homophobia that still exists in America than about anything Jenny Jones and her staff did.

In any event, the question is fairly asked: Could anything like that happen on our show? Probably not like that. We tell our guests ahead of time if there's going to be a surprise and what the parameters of that surprise are. For example, before guests appear on a "surprise" show, they are given a list of 21 possible scenarios that might be the surprise. If they don't agree to every single possibility, they can't be on the show. I'm told that usually the one that is the most feared by the guys is that their girlfriend (or wife) might be pregnant! I can see why that might be scarier than finding out that your girlfriend is really a guy!

After looking at and signing this document of possible surprises, obviously a guest couldn't come back and say, "Gee, I didn't know that this surprise was a possibility."

I know what you're thinking: How could anyone put my name on money!

Well, in an effort to cut down on the expense of paying for meals at hotels, which could often total in excess of $150 to $200, we came up with another idea. We give what's referred to as "Jerry Dollars" to use for food at the hotels where the guests are staying. It's our version of "Monopoly money."

There have been some memorable incidents involving guests and their hotel rooms. I don't know what it is about staying in a hotel that gives some of our guests the impression that they can act like rambunctious children, but for some of them, I guess they look at these few days away from home as a temporary (in some cases) loss of sanity. My producers have had to deal with all sorts of grief from guests, but here are some of the most unbelievable stories.

Sheila Rosenbaum,

PRODUCER 1993–1997

There was trouble at a hotel one night because one of our guests decided he should throw water balloons out of his window at people. Hotels are very particular about which of our guests can stay where. Our guests, frankly, have been kicked out of so many hotels in Chicago that we're basically limited as to where our guests can stay. I call it, "Rent-a-Car Syndrome." People don't really care about rental cars, and to that degree, some of the people on our show don't care about the rooms we put them in. Some of these people have never been away from home before, or to the airport, on a plane, let alone ever stayed in a hotel, so they just don't act like normal people during their stay. They look at it as an all-expense-paid trip to Chicago and a chance to act loose and crazy.

Annette Grundy,

SENIOR PRODUCER 1991–1997

We once had a guest who was literally half of a human body from the waist up. He walked on his hands. He had suffered a birth defect when he was born where his spine wasn't properly formed. If you took a tall water bottle, that's just about how high he was off of the ground. When he sat on a chair, it looked almost like an illusion, because all you could see was this guy from the waist up, and it appeared as if the lower part of his body was mysteriously hidden in the chair. This guy is in his hotel lobby when I get a panicked phone call from the hotel saying that there had been an "incident."

Apparently, there had been a meeting taking place at the hotel, and it adjourned into the lobby where this guest was. All of these regular-height people came out of the conference room, and not one person saw our guest. He completely freaked out and jumped up onto a luggage cart, where he proceeded to swing himself around the top of the cart and terrorize these other people. They were all horrified and somewhat panicked by our guest's appearance and outright display of anger. I had to calm the desk clerk down and convince our guest that it wasn't really great behavior on his part to terrorize the other guests in the hotel.

Another great story involves a waiter who delivered room service to a mother and daughter. The daughter was pregnant, and when the waiter knocked on the door, both the mother and daughter were standing there stark naked. They asked him if he would come inside and take pictures of them. I'm not exactly sure why the waiter complained, but he did, and we had to remind the mother and daughter that they couldn't do this to the employees of the hotel.

There are guests who will literally take anything from a hotel that isn't bolted down. We've had to replace sheets, towels, drapes, the iron, the blow dryers, full minibars—you name it. In fact, we won't allow hotels to offer minibars in the rooms to our guests anymore. We just didn't have the money in our production budget to cover the enormous charges.

And one of the grossest stories I have about a guest in a hotel involves a family that stayed in a room together and defecated all over the room: in the closet, smeared on the drapes, and all over the walls. To this day, I don't know who did it, but someone from that family sure trashed this four-star room.

Rachelle Consiglio,
SENIOR PRODUCER 1995–PRESENT

I had one show that turned into a total hotel nightmare. It was a show called, "My Lover Is Cheating." This show was going to be great. All of the parties involved were very passionate about the situation. We flew them out separately, as is customary in these situations so we don't have them fighting on the plane ahead of time and lose the intensity of the situation on the stage.

In cases like this, we usually fly the two-timing man with the woman who is less eager to do the show so that she will come. The other woman, who is most interested in the confrontation, is usually okay to travel alone because she wants to come to the show to let him have it on national TV.

Once in Chicago, the man sometimes has to go back and forth to each of the women's hotel rooms to keep them happy so they will show up at the show the next day. The men usually don't find much of a problem in doing this because this is what they are doing outside the show anyway.

Both of the women on this show had children with the man and both wanted him to themselves. As always, we had booked the two women in separate hotel rooms far away from each other to avoid any preshow confrontations. This time however, that plan didn't work out. The woman who was not staying with the man before the show got really drunk and called every hotel in Chicago until she discovered where the other two were staying.

She went charging over to the other hotel in a drunken rage, found their room, and literally broke the door down, hinges and all. The hotel called their security, and when they could not control her, they called in the cops and she was arrested for damage to property.

I missed this interplay by about ten minutes so I couldn't prevent her from being thrown in jail. Unfortunately, once a guest has actually been booked, it's out of our hands and they're at the mercy of the courts.

She spent 28 hours in jail before she was finally released. She was really angry with me and I tried to explain to her that it was not my fault. She was the one who got drunk and broke down the door and got arrested, but she didn't see it that way. Anyway, by the time she actually got to the show, jail had taken all the steam out of her and she had nothing left to say onstage and the show was a dud. Too bad, the energy had been there two days before when we flew them out.

Just one other note about that show. The hotel where the door was broken down won't let us book guests there anymore because one of their regular guests was in the room next door and he cancelled his account with them that night.

Conversely, if we feel that a hotel doesn't treat our guests respectfully, we address the issue immediately with their management. Occasionally, someone might see that a person is checking in as a "*Jerry Springer Show*" guest, and they might get a little less service or a little more attitude. We don't go for that. We want all of our guests to be treated with respect and with the same courteous service as any other guest would normally receive. So on the day of the taping, guests are brought to the studio and they are placed in a waiting room that is often referred to as "the Green Room." A PA (production assistant) will have them sign a release, which is also videotaped to ensure authenticity.

The audience is ushered in and handled by our "audience coordinator," Lisa Farina. Her job is to make sure that the seats are full and there is a good balance struck for each taping.

Lisa Farina,
AUDIENCE COORDINATOR 1995–PRESENT

When people call in for tickets, I have a particular set of rules that I go by before I send them. First of all, people call from all over Europe and the United States to get tickets for the show. I don't give tickets out however unless they can tell me the dates they are going to be in town and can give me a local number where they can be reached when they are here. I do this so that I don't send out too many tickets to people who are not going to show up.

The rules are that you must be 18 years or older to attend. No shorts, baseball hats, or white clothing is allowed (the white clothing looks bad on camera). When more than one ticket is requested, I ask that they come with an equal number of men and women because I don't want the audience to be all one sex. The ideal audience for me is a well-dressed, diverse, and well-balanced group. The only other rule I have when seating the audience is no older people in the front row. You sometimes have to be able to move pretty quickly up there, and I wouldn't want anybody hurt.

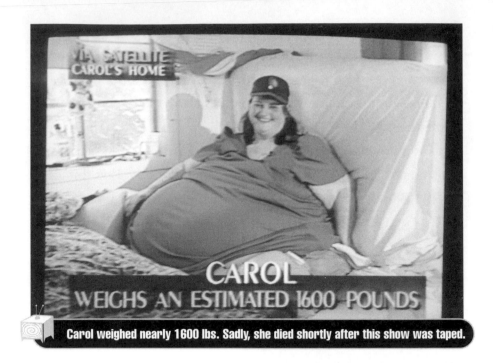

CAROL
WEIGHS AN ESTIMATED 1600 POUNDS

Carol weighed nearly 1600 lbs. Sadly, she died shortly after this show was taped.

Guests on *"The Jerry Springer Show"* come in all sizes, shapes, and species. There's no doubt that the physical appeal of a guest can leave an indelible impression on you, good or bad. We're not a judgmental show; so our motto is, and has always been, "Come as you are."

Our producers usually ask for pictures of our guests before they come on the show. But there have been times where guests show up, and they look nothing like the photo they sent us. And that's okay, because we have a full-time hair and makeup person, dentist, and a huge wardrobe closet full of all sorts of clothing choices.

Our producers usually get a physical description of a guest over the phone, and the accuracy of the information they provide might be slightly askew. Sometimes even a picture doesn't always paint a real story. We've had people send in pictures of friends, claiming it as themselves. We've had drag queens

Red is traditionally our most popular color.

describe themselves by saying, "When I dress like a woman, no one can tell I'm really a man." And yet, when they show up for their taping, they look like a bearded Hercules.

Some guests show up and have only a few or even no teeth, and perhaps they're self-conscious about that. So we have a resident dentist, Dr. Sood, who by now has probably bought a house on the beach with the money he has made from *"The Jerry Springer Show"*!

If a guest needs wardrobe, we've got a closetful of clothes. We have dresses in all shapes and sizes, shirts, ties, and lots of shoes, especially high heels.

Ginger Damato, our makeup person, has had to endure some real challenges over the years. She's usually the one member of our staff who has to deal with the guests almost as much as the producers. And, in some cases, it takes a little finessing on her part.

Ginger Damato,
MAKEUP ARTIST 1992–PRESENT

You never know what you're going to find behind the Green Room doors. I've seen it all. One morning, just like the rest, I walk into the Green Room and I'm introduced to Lori and Dori. Lori and Dori are conjoined twins connected by the head around the eye area. Lori stands about 5'8" and her sister is smaller, so she rides around on a wheeled seat next to her. The smaller one is playing the guitar and singing a little. I was a little shocked when I met them because no one had told me ahead of time that they were coming. I wanted to make them feel as comfortable as

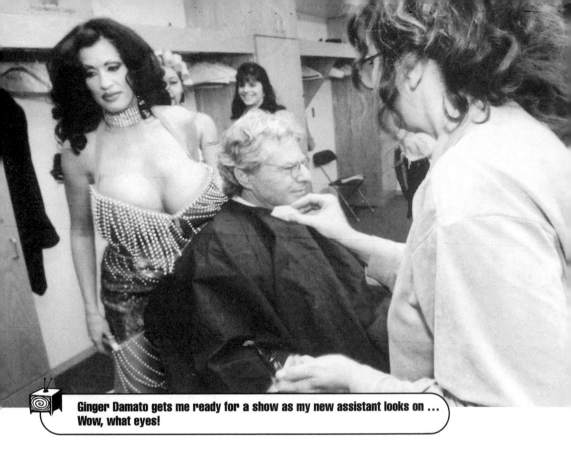

Ginger Damato gets me ready for a show as my new assistant looks on ... Wow, what eyes!

I could, so I said to Dori, "Oh, I love country-western music," as she is strumming away on her guitar.

They came into the makeup room, which is attached to the Green Room, and I started to get them ready for the show. Dori wouldn't talk to me directly. She would say to her sister, "Tell her to make my hair look like Reba's." And I would say, "I can hear you, Dori." But she just wouldn't acknowledge me directly. I never found out why.

By the time they came on the show for the sixth time, she certainly hadn't lost any of her interest in country music. In fact, she now liked to be called "Little Reba" as in Reba MacIntyre, the country-western singer.

I think the first indication the show had changed was when

Conjoined twins, Lori and Dori have been on our show a number of times. Dori (on the right) is an aspiring country-western singer like me. They are both truly inspirational.

this woman came up to me and asked me to powder her butt. That was a first for me. A week later another girl, who was to take a shower onstage completely nude, asked me quite seriously if I could paint on some pubic hair for her. You see, my job used to be a typical job for television. A little powder on the face, some blush, and away they go. Not anymore! Now it's more of a total makeover job.

One time I had a man in the makeup room who was coming out of the closet on the show for the very first time and he wanted to wear an evening gown. He wanted to look "pretty." So we made him up and got him into this beautiful low-cut gown. The problem was that he was as hairy as they come; I mean a real carpet on his back.

He looked at himself in the mirror and started to get very distressed and said that he couldn't go out there looking the way he did. So I suggested to my assistant that we shave his back. But she didn't think this would work out well because it would leave stubble. So we eventually decided to "Nair" his back instead.

It took awhile to get him ready for the stage but when we were done, he felt pretty and went out onstage a new man.

As an artist, and as an employee of *"The Jerry Springer Show,"* I always have to be prepared for a challenge. In fact, we recently did a show called, "I Married a Horse." On this show not only did I have to disguise the guests, who were romantically involved with their pets, I had to disguise the pets too. Five minutes before show time I was applying mascara to the blond eyelashes of a Great Dane. I think I really need to see a psychiatrist.

Don't we all? In fact, we get a group rate for all of our employees at *"The Jerry Springer Show."* Actually, we do have a resident therapist known as Dr. Butterworth. We use him regularly on the show to help counsel some of our guests, though he often comes out and just yells at everyone for being so out of touch. He's become something of a cult figure to our fans.

Some guests choose to wear a disguise on our show; and to

Affiliate Relations, Betsy Bergman, and I, backstage at the House of Blues in Chicago before I take the stage to perform "Dr. Talk."

make it easier for them, we supply everything they might need. We've had characters in clown outfits, masks, wigs, glasses, and hats. Some people wear fake beards and mustaches. One of our classic episodes involves two characters, Rufus and Trenae, who came out in disguises, bad ones, looking more like Stevie Wonder and the Artist formally known as "Prince." It was a show from February 1994 called "I Need to Tell You This!"

Betsy Bergman, who is in charge of affiliate relations for our show and who is probably the only person on earth who has seen every single episode of *"The Jerry Springer Show,"* says this is her absolute favorite show.

Betsy Bergman,

AFFILIATE RELATIONS 1994–PRESENT

My favorite show of all time is "I Need to Tell You This!" We had these guests on, Raleen and Torrace, who were getting married. But before they walked down the aisle, Torrace had something he needed to tell Raleen. So there they are on the set when Torrace confesses he's been cheating on Raleen, who completely flips out. It turns out he was cheating on her with her best friend, who comes out and admits to Raleen she's having an affair with her fiancé. The women start yelling at each other, asking, "What's your definition of a best friend?" and "How could you do this to me?"

It was an amazing and intense segment.

But Torrace wasn't quite through with his confession. It turns out that he was also sleeping with his best friend, Trenae, who is a man! The women were completely shocked. So now Trenae comes out and he turns to Torrace and says, "I'm cheating on you with my best friend." Who, as it turns out, is a guy named Rufus. Both Trenae and Rufus were in these ridiculous disguises. They became like characters out of a movie. The energy and conflict between everyone on the stage was really incredible. It was *Springer* at its best!

Another thing we provide our guests is props. If someone comes out and they are going to do an erotic dance, it might help create a better visual if they have a feather boa. Maybe they need a portable pool to stand in while someone applies chocolate pudding all over their body—no problem, we've got one of those. . . .

Rufus and Trenae with Dr. Dre and Ed Lover.

Say you want to propose to your lover but you don't have an engagement ring. No problem, we've got a drawer full. We can even provide the clergy to perform the ceremony. We can give you a teddy bear to hold on to or flowers to present as a peace offering, though more times than not, someone is always getting clobbered by the bouquet.

Now, just before we tape the show, Todd Schultz, our stage manager—and he often doubles as security—warms up the audience and lays down the ground rules. He explains that no one in the audience is allowed to shout out anything that will promote fighting between the guests. As an audience member, you're basically limited to booing, hissing, "oohs and ahhs," and, of course, the preverbal, "Jer-ry! Jer-ry! Jer-ry!"

This was supposed to be a cooking show. Something went terribly wrong.

Our stage manager, Todd, warms up the audience before I come out. Pictured here, he is stumped when an audience member asks him to spell "Todd."

Once Todd lays down the ground rules, I come out to do a five-minute shtick. Yes, my jokes are corny, but hey, I'm a corny guy! Every year at our staff wrap party, I promise new jokes for the next season. Haven't changed one word in seven years . . . probably never will.

Once the taping is over, I stay in the studio, sign autographs, take pictures, and shake hands with the audience as they're leaving.

For our guests, we provide transportation back home, and the rest, as they say, is history. There are stories of guests who have had a confrontation on our show and then run into each other at the airport, where, sadly, it starts all over again. Unfortunately, once a guest leaves our show, they're under the jurisdiction of the Chicago Police Department, and really at their mercy.

In fact, long-term consequences can also prevail. We once had a woman on our show who admitted to having an affair with a 16-year-old boy (she was around 40), and when she got home and the show aired, she was arrested for statutory rape! She did not blame our show for her arrest; and, interestingly, she wanted to do a follow-up show from jail, but the authorities in New York wouldn't let us shoot her from prison. We even had a guest on our show who was recently featured on the television show *America's Most Wanted*. I made an appearance on their show to help find this guy.

Oftentimes guests will check in with their producers after they've been on to give an update or generally just to say hello. Most of the time it's friendly chitchat, but occasionally, there is a guest who thinks that their 15 minutes of fame isn't quite over.

I insist on meeting every member of the audience after each show. If I'd come all this way to see them, I'm sure they'd extend the same courtesy.

They become obsessive and have been known to make threats if they aren't invited back to the show. The producers sometimes refer to this as "guest residue" that won't go away. They want to talk about their show, and if they did a good job, and how do they think the audience liked them, and did I say anything, etc, etc, etc. . . .

My producers tell me that return guests are sometimes the most difficult guests to work with because they are the most demanding. They've been through the drill at least once before, so they know what to expect, and some of them they want the "star" treatment. They make crazy requests, such as flying in family members or insisting on other perks in order to appear. When that happens, we usually end up finding another guest. Some guests grow so attached to members of our staff, they're thinking—*date.*

Sheila Rosenbaum,
PRODUCER 1993–1997

I was brought out on a show we did that was actually an update show called "Viewers Confront Past Guests!" And as a surprise to me, one of our viewers developed a crush on me! I guess he'd seen me on television on another show and he wrote a love poem that he read to me, live, in front of everyone! It was something like: "Roses are red, violets are blue. I turned on the TV and fell in love with you!"

And suddenly, Jerry asks me what I think of this guy. What was I supposed to say? "He's a total dork?" Needless to say, Jerry, who is a huge practical joker, says to this guy, "Make sure

Sheila Rosenbaum on the job... tough work, but someone's got to do it.

you have her back early because she's got to work tomorrow!"

The guy actually says to Jerry, "How early?"

I really thought Jerry was going to pawn me off on this guy, who, by the way, was arrested immediately after the show because apparently he had gotten into a fight at the hotel the night before. The police were waiting to take him in immediately after the taping!

Strippers and transsexuals like to walk around naked. They're very uninhibited. And it's funny, because I have noticed that transsexuals all have this same odor to them, too. I think it's from the hormones they use, but it smells like they're PMS-ing for a month! It's a memorable smell, that's for sure.

RINGMASTER!   **139**

I often hear from my critics that we "exploit" our guests on *"The Jerry Springer Show."* My response is simple: we don't, and I work to make sure we never do. However, to be honest, I used to be in the business of exploitation. You see, I did the news. For ten years I anchored the news in Cincinnati, and like all newscasts and newspapers, we were often horribly exploitative.

Every night we would jam the microphone into the face of someone who didn't want to be on camera—someone coming out of a courthouse, a family involved in a horrible tragedy—and we'd report the story regardless of the fact that it might hurt, or embarrass, or humiliate that person or their family.

Think about it. News hurts people every day. News hurts people without their permission, without their consent, and all because stations or newspapers want to beat their competition, or win the ratings, get the story first, and make big profits. It's a ruthless business. News will never say, "Gee, if this story will hurt your career or your marriage or embarrass your children, we won't run it." Bull. If it makes a great headline or a great scoop, if it'll draw viewers to the 11:00 news during sweeps month, to hell with the pain it inflicts or the exploitation of the people it bludgeoned in the lead story. This is about ratings after all.

Now I know. These people who call themselves "journalists" will rationalize their behavior with self-justifying claims of "Well, it's news. We have a duty to inform the public. The people need to know." Sounds great, but it's mostly, and sadly, not true.

Please know that 90 percent of what the news reports, we don't *need* to know. We may *want* to know it, and we may be *interested* in knowing it, but we don't *need* to know it. We need to know if we're at war, or if the water we drink is poisoned, or if our taxes are going up. But we don't need to know if there's been a car accident across town. We surely don't need two years of nonstop coverage of the O. J. Simpson trial, whose venomous act affected no one but the immediate families involved. We don't need to know about Marv Albert, or who's dating whom or divorcing whom. And I still haven't figured out why it's any of our business if President Clinton's been unfaithful in his marriage.

I'm not suggesting we're not interested in any of these stories. I'm just wondering whether we actually need to know about them. And, of course, the answer is, we don't—particularly when you weigh the deep pain visited upon these people and their families versus our shameless addiction simply to have our gossip quotas filled. Let's face it, news seriously exploits and hurts people every day—not *"The Jerry Springer Show!"*

Now I can already hear your response. "The nerve," you say. "How can you, Jerry, who puts on this wild and crazy talk show every day, be charging news with exploitation? What do you think you do?"

Well, there is a major, major difference.

You see, our show is purely voluntary. While news reports damage people without their consent every day, on our show we never put anybody on unless they desperately want to be on. They call us. They go through interview after interview. They come to Chicago. We don't pay them, and it's their own choice to appear on our show. They can wear a disguise, use a phony name, and we won't permit them to talk about anyone who isn't there to defend themselves. If there's a surprise, the person is told ahead of time what the parameters of that surprise are. And only if the guest agrees to do it will we do it. They can say whatever they want, refuse to talk about whatever they don't want to talk about; they can back out of the show at any time. This is 100 percent different than the assault of a news report, which isn't voluntary at all.

On our show we never ever report on a person who doesn't want to be on or doesn't want to be talked about. Would news ever agree to those rules? Yeah, right. Would the news ever agree not to talk about anybody unless they had their written permission or unless the public had a clearly demonstrative need to know? Not in our lifetime. No. News will continue to exploit people, hurt people, and ruin people's lives. We see it happening on local and national news all the time. We know that's the truth—and we do nothing about it. It's a lot easier to complain about talk shows, particularly mine.

It's just a thought. . . .

A particular story comes to mind when thinking about whether we "exploit" our guests. We did a show on a baby that weighed 70 pounds. His parents were approached by every talk show on the air, and they were very concerned about their son, Zack, being mistreated and exploited by the media. Annette Grundy was the producer of this show and she came to me and explained the parents' concern, which I clearly understood, both as a journalist and as a parent. I decided that I would speak to them myself and assure them that if they agreed to come on our show, they would be treated with the utmost respect . . . and they were. They agreed to do our show. I held Zack and played with him like I would with any other baby. He was really sweet, and in spite of his abnormal size, quite normal.

After that show, I arranged to have all of the medical testing Zack needed. We've followed Zack and his development over the last few years, and even did a second show with the entire family from Jamaica.

That's Zack, the 70-lb. baby. We had his exclusive story.

A lot of people have wondered how the "Jer-ry! Jer-ry! Jer-ry!" chanting got started. Actually it was a spin-off from the "Go, Ricki! Go, Ricki!" that Ricki Lake's audience used to chant when she came out. When our audience started chanting, "Jer-ry! Jer-ry!" Richard Dominick realized that keeping the chant in the show was a good way to keep the energy up in the room. Here's Richard's own recollection on why he felt we needed, of all things, to have the audience members chant my name.

Richard Dominick,

PRODUCER/EXECUTIVE PRODUCER 1991–PRESENT

When I took over as the executive producer in 1994, our viewing audience was nothing like it is today. The Multimedia executives gave me the show in April of '94 and, basically, gave me the responsibility of raising the ratings. My job was to figure out how to get more people to watch. I knew one thing for sure . . . the show had to be interesting to watch, even if the sound was turned off. So if someone were channel surfing, as soon as they would hit *"The Jerry Springer Show,"* it had to grab their attention.

The first thing I did was put his name in the corner of the screen for the entire show. I figured, at the very least, people would get to know Jerry's name. That graphic is called a "bug." No one was using a bug at the time, so it was innovative and we were the first show to use it. Today, of course, you see a network graphic in the corner of every show you watch. It has become brand identification. All I wanted was for people to know who Jerry was. The graphic helped. So did the fact that the audience had started chanting, "Jer-ry! Jer-ry!" in and out of every segment. In fact, they chant it now every time something is happening onstage. We'll ask you to leave if you yell out anything else. You can say, "ooh and ahhh," but other than that it's, "Jer-ry! Jer-ry!" that emanates from the airwaves. No, "Hit em . . . " or cursing. The bottom line is that I knew I had to create a way to use the name "Jerry Springer" in every tense. And it worked! Today he is a noun, a verb, and an adjective. Today, Jerry can't walk through an airport or down a street without hearing, "Jer-ry! Jer-ry! Jer-ry!" which, coincidentally, surprises him even today.

It's easy for Richard to tell that story because no one's shouting, "Rich-ard! Rich-ard! Rich-ard!" out at him all of the time! It's funny though, because I've gotten used to it, so it doesn't bother me at all. In fact, I recently went to a New York Yankees game and a fight broke out on the field between the players. All of the sudden, the fans in the stands started chanting, "Jer-ry! Jer-ry! Jer-ry!?!"

Richard Dominick realized that our show titles are some of the most interesting, if not the most clever, on the air today. But if you tuned in late, it might take you a few minutes to figure out what the topic was for that particular day. So in an absolute stroke of genius, Richard decided to add the show title on the screen and let it live there for an entire show so that you would always know exactly what you were watching.

Finally, to help create a

If you like my show, here's the man to thank. Richard Dominick is the brains behind "The Jerry Springer Show" as well as a close friend.

RINGMASTER!

better identification for our show—a trademark, so to speak—
we end each segment with what's referred to as "a tease." A
tease is something that keeps a viewer tuned in. For example,
you may hear me say something like the following, "Jenny
doesn't know it, but her boyfriend has been secretly seeing
someone else and he's coming out next to tell her! So stay
tuned!" Or you might hear something like, "Coming up, you'll
be shocked at what our next guest wants to reveal to his family.
Stay with us!" When you hear me say something to that effect,
basically you're being teased by me not to change the channel . . .
and hopefully you'll keep watching!

Linda Shafran works tirelessly handling the publicity for our
show (her job has gotten a little more demanding in the last
year!) and often travels with me when I need to make a personal
appearance. She's gotten used to being around me, which is
more than I can say for myself!

Linda Shafran,
PUBLICITY DEPARTMENT 1995–PRESENT

I remember walking through O'Hare Airport with Jerry once and
everyone kept saying, "Did you see who's here?" People were
stopping in their tracks just to get a glimpse of Jerry. Everyone
was pointing and whispering, and I noticed that Jerry was turn-
ing around too! He finally turned to me and seriously asked,
"Who is everyone talking about? It must be someone famous.
Let's see."

Jerry hadn't a clue that it was him!

Eric Olson writes our on-air promos for every show. His job is to make sure you're enticed to watch our show. He's a very funny and talented writer, with a gift for twisting the absurd, crazy, outrageousness of our show. Here's how Eric describes his job.

Eric Olson,
ON-AIR PROMOTIONS 1996–PRESENT

I think I have the best job on the show. Since the show is fun, the producers and the powers that be just let me punt. I don't have to stick to the rigid mold of what a promo usually is. I get

On-air Promotions, Eric Olson, and Public Relations, Laurie Fried.

to have fun creating basically what I call these short, structural films that are one big gag. Every time I come up with a stupid idea, they say, "Do it!"

A good example of what I do is when I did a radio promo that was really cheesy. It had a happy announcer with happy music playing in the background. And the announcer comes on and says, "When you tune into *'The Jerry Springer Show,'* you're tun- ing into America's favorite hour of feel-good TV. It's about friend- ships, it's about love, and occasionally it's about fucked-up weirdos saying shit to embarrass the crap out of the people they fucked with." Of course, all of the curse words had to be bleeped out, so it resembled a pretty typical *Springer* episode.

Eric also keeps an archive of his favorite names of actual people who call into our show to be on as guests. Just for fun, I thought you might like to see a sampling.

Hey, if you're pregnant, you don't need to buy that "Baby Names" book. I think you'll find the most creative and current list of names right here!

Cool Names

TAHNEE	TEKA	VERETHA
NAKIYA	MSTODI	PRECIOUS
ZAKIYA	KHADIJAH	LINDELL
DIAMOND	PUMPKIN	THURMAN
NAJA	TREMONT	TYRE
DEJA	JUICEY	LAKENYA
LASETTA	MICA	WINTER
LA TANYA	MOON	AMENE
KALYSIA	JUSTICE	TIREE
NAIROBI	MEISH	JUBA
SHAWNTEL	IMANI	ODETTA

RAHSAAN	SPARKLES	SHOLA
EDTCHRESS	TUGGIE	TWANA
LUBERTHA	REXANIUS	LATOYA
LAQUITA	GOLDIE	AISHA
VERSELL	CALTONE	TAMESHA
RUFUS	ZANDRA	BRAETTA
TRENAE	HEAVEN	RAZBERRY
AMIKA	SUGAR	ROOSTER
ISIS	TIESA	PEPPER
CHAKA	TICO	UNSEL
UNSELL	SHONDE	SHAHLELAH
PEACHES	STARLA	
CHANGO	GWAIN	
RAMZI	CHOPPER	
TAVISH	SHENIDIA	

NINE
Putting the "T" & "A" Back in TALK

Jerry Springer is the patron saint of <u>Talk</u> <u>Soup</u>.
—JOHN HENSON
HOST, <u>TALK</u> <u>SOUP</u>, E! ENTERTAINMENT TELEVISION

The best stories to share about this silly circus maximus known as *"The Jerry Springer Show"* are the ones I simply cannot tell. Not because there's something to hide, but rather because most of what occurs happens before it all ever gets to me. The night before a show I get a brief outline—perhaps a one-paragraph summary of the show: who the guests are and what the truth is. That's all I want to know about a show. That way, going into the program without a script, without knowing what I'm going to ask or what the guests are going to say, I can be much more spontaneous, much more surprised in a segment. I can react just as you, the viewer, does.

So you can see, except for my Final Thought, most of the work is done by my staff—some 80 or so people who work extremely hard to put together the 200 shows we tape a year. It would be an injustice for me to try and put their stories and experiences into my own words. Oh, there're still some stories I can tell you firsthand, and I will, but theirs are the ones that enticed you to buy this book. These are the "behind the scenes" stories that surprised even me. Consider this your all-access backstage pass to *"The Jerry Springer Show."*

Richard Dominick started off as a line producer during our first season. He was the crazy one responsible for pushing our limits as far as he could without getting us into too much trouble. Here's Richard in his own words on some of his most memorable shows:

Richard Dominick,
PRODUCER/EXECUTIVE PRODUCER 1991–PRESENT

I had three "dream shows" that I really wanted as a producer. The first one was when we had to literally cut a hole in the side of this house because the 860-pound man living inside was so fat he couldn't fit through the door. His name was Denny, and he lived in Hamilton, Ohio. He was having a lot of trouble breathing, so the show agreed to get him to a hospital for help.

We had to break through a brick wall in the side of his house because we had to make an opening large enough for Denny to fit through. I remember Jerry was helping to knock down the wall and a big chunk of brick hit him on the head, but he was fine. (When we rebuilt Denny's wall, we built him doors that were big enough for him to walk through and also built him a deck.)

There was no stretcher that was strong enough to hold him,

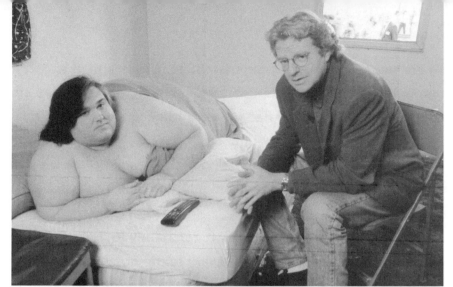

Denny Welch first appeared on our show as Eartha Quake, the world's largest transsexual. Years later, he ballooned to over 800 lbs. We had to cut a hole through a wall in his house to get him out and to a hospital for tests.

so we had to use a door from the house. It took 8 men to carry him out. They were bodybuilders from a local gym. He was so enormous and heavy, we had to use a truck scale to weigh him because a regular scale wouldn't work. We weighed the ambulance at a truck weigh station along the highway before we put him in it and then again afterward with him in it. The difference was his weight.

Paramedics had to monitor him constantly to make sure he didn't have a heart attack on the way to the hospital. Once we got there, the team of physicians had to use what's called a polar bear table to examine Denny. (A polar bear table is what veterinarians use to operate on polar bears and the Cincinnati zoo happened to be one of the only zoos in the country that had one, so they loaned it to the hospital to help out Denny and the doctors with his examination.)

Our goal was to ultimately get Denny the proper medical attention and help him get into a diet clinic, which we ultimately accomplished. Because of our episode featuring Denny, HBO offered to do a special on him and Richard Simmons even called him up to offer his support.

A funny thing happened at the hospital though. Jerry had to go to the bathroom and accidentally walked in on a nurse who was using the facility. She screamed, he screamed, and all I heard was a door slam. When she came out, she said to one of our producers, "The funniest thing just happened. I think Jerry Springer just walked in on me going to the bathroom!" She was so excited to see him she said she didn't mind and that she couldn't wait to tell everybody she knew.

Speaking of hospitals, another dream show I wanted to do was about a woman in labor. And like many of the shows we have done in the past, we very often don't know where it's going until we're there, and this was one of them. The show was originally about a pregnant woman who was going to confront her husband's mistress on our show.

Well, as only *"The Jerry Springer Show"* could do, our pregnant guest went into labor just before the taping of the show! Apparently she had been fighting with her husband that morning and the stress had triggered her contractions. We had decided that we should cancel the show, but the pregnant woman, in the true spirit of show business, decided that "the show must go on," despite the fact that she was now in labor and at the hospital. She said, "I came all the way to Chicago and I'm not going to let any other woman be with my man!"

We tried to stop her, but she insisted. So she checked herself out of the hospital and showed up at our studios wearing her slippers and hospital gown! We brought a team of paramedics to the studio to keep an eye on her throughout the taping. She would start having contractions in the middle of her sentences, but she was going to confront that mistress, come hell or high water. Every time we would go to a commercial break, out came the paramedics. After the show she went back to the hospital, where she stayed in labor for another two days.

She came back two months after she gave birth for a follow-up show, and her husband was still seeing his mistress. He didn't want to give either of the women up. He figured, "Why would I? I've got two women!" The second the mistress came out on stage, though, the formerly pregnant woman let loose all of her anger and frustration: she pounded her.

I also wanted to do a show about a transvestite who'd gotten another woman pregnant, and I am pleased to tell you that recently that dream has come true. One of our favorite guests, Brittaney, a transvestite, recently returned to our show to

announce that she had impregnated her lesbian lover and that
she was going to become a "dad."

Well, we all have our dreams. I'm not sure mine were ever like
that. . . .

Annette Grundy came to our show as a young, hard-working
producer, while we were still shooting out of Cincinnati. She
had a kind of connection and rapport with Richard that worked
like a well-oiled machine. Even though she left the show last
season, she is still very much in our hearts, and we miss her
spark.

Annette Grundy,
PRODUCER/SR. PRODUCER 1991–1997

One of my favorite stories about a past guest is what I call "the
Wolf Story." It's about a stripper who came on the show, and
while she was in the Green Room, she would ask every single
person if she could show them her "wolf." I mean she asked
everyone from the soundman to Ginger, the makeup artist.

It turned out that her "wolf" was a tattoo drawn from her
stomach down and around her entire crotch area. When she
would pull up the skin on her stomach, her clitoris would pop
out like a tongue. We were all like, "Thanks for sharing, wolf
lady." The rest of the day the buzz around the office was, "Did
you see the wolf?"

But believe it or not, my most memorable show—the one
with which I'm most proud to be associated—was the show that

featured two young kids who had contracted the HIV virus. One day I was looking through the *Star* magazine and I saw a picture of this little boy and little girl in a tuxedo and a wedding dress. They had just gotten married, and I was blown away because they both had AIDS and wanted to fulfill their dream of getting married before they died. I had to find these kids because I wanted to get them on the show, which I did. I even had them renew their vows.

Hydeia, who is like an angel on earth and whom I love very much, had been born with AIDS. Her mother was a prostitute who gave her up two days after she was born. Her adopted mother didn't find out about the disease until Hydeia was three years old. The doctors didn't think she would live beyond the age of five, but she did. The doctors then figured that she

RINGMASTER!   **157**

wouldn't make it to her tenth birthday. But again, she did. And just this year she turned fourteen. Her mother is an amazing woman who has taught Hydeia about the power of love.

Tyler, the little boy we featured on the show, also had AIDS, and it was incredible to see these young kids be so strong and brave. I have a special place in my heart for them. But most of all, with all of the craziness we produced over the years, this was by far the most important show for me.

I have to admit that every now and then it is nice to bring a story of hope to the airwaves. Hydeia and Tyler have visited the show several times since their wedding, and to surprise them

The two children pictured here are Hydeia and Tyler. They both maintain positive attitudes despite their struggles with HIV. We surprised them with a performance by Hydeia's favorite band, Naughty By Nature.

we brought in some of their favorites—the rap group Naughty by Nature, and, to demonstrate the range of their tastes, Billy Ray Cyrus.

In fairness, Burt Dubrow is the man I give credit to for launching this lunacy. It was Burt who pioneered those first days on the air in Cincinnati. I spoke to him as I was writing this book, and he reminded me of some of our earlier moments when the show was slightly tamer than it is today. Here he is in his own words.

Burt Dubrow,
EXECUTIVE PRODUCER 1991–1997

I always wanted to produce shows that people would watch even if they had the sound turned off on their television sets. Once we started getting beyond the softer topics we'd originally started with, it opened the door to get a little risqué. One of our first efforts at introducing strippers to our show was called "I Want to Be an Exotic Dancer!"

We had contestants write in letters that were 25 words or less on why they wanted to be an exotic dancer. We brought all of the winners to Chicago and did a remote shoot from a downtown strip club. We also had the contestants' husbands fly in, who would get to see their wives strip for the first time during our taping.

We gave the women a crash course in erotic dancing, taught by a genuine stripper. In fact, we had the real stripper come out first and she took off her top, which we obviously could not air. But I remember that as our first nude edit.

Our wrap party, June 1996. I had just suggested to Burt Dubrow that he buy a round of drinks.

It was a great show! Everyone was having a good time . . . especially Jerry. Of course, there was this other side to Jerry—perhaps his real side—his serious, political side. For example, I remember how excited Jerry got about interviewing Oliver North. Jerry is a real avid political follower and for him to be able to interview this American icon—hero or villain, depending on your perspective—well, that was more exciting than any other show we had done at the time.

Of course, today Oliver North would never get booked as a guest on the show because it's just so different now, but back then, that made good television.

I guess the show I most remember though was the one where we had the crew of *48 Hours* backstage covering us. They were doing a piece on talk show producers and I was being featured in the segment. At the time I was the executive producer of *Sally Jessy Raphael* and *"The Jerry Springer Show."* I would often tape Sally in the mornings, which taped out of New York, and then hop on a plane to Chicago to do Jerry in the afternoons.

On this particular day, *48 Hours* had their cameras rolling all day as I went through this routine. We had booked what we referred to as a "Klan" show . . . but I never anticipated the outcome. What happened was what I refer to as "the first fight" on *"The Jerry Springer Show."*

There was an angry confrontation between the Klan members and members of the Antidefamation League, who were also guests that day. The confrontation disintegrated into an all-out brawl. At the time there was no such thing as fighting during a talk show. In fact, the only fight I had ever heard of had been on *Geraldo.* So there was no thought given to the fact that there might be a slugfest. But there was, and I was so excited by it that I started jumping up and down with my hands up in the air, screaming, "This is terrific! We're going to be on the news! We're going to be national!" And as I said this, I realized, "Oh, my God . . . " I had totally forgotten that I had on a microphone and that the *48 Hours* cameras were rolling . . . on me! My heart sank, because although I wanted people to notice us, I figured I could really get into trouble for this. I knew this was a new frontier for talk. But I sure didn't want to hurt the show, and I knew this kind of publicity couldn't be good . . . or at least that's what I thought at the time. I immediately called the people at Multimedia and explained what had happened. Their response was, "We trust you, Burt."

We decided to let our show air unedited. Unfortunately, so did *48 Hours.* I thought for sure that Bob Turner, who was then the president of Multimedia, was going to have my neck: but to my surprise, he didn't. Whatever . . . the footage of me jumping up and down like an idiot was the footage they used to promo the *48 Hours* show all night long! I have asked myself over and over since then . . . why couldn't they have been using a lousy cameraman that day?

In addition to creating and executive producing the *Sally Jessy Raphael Show* for 10 years and getting my show started, Burt continued to consult on a whole range of talk shows and today remains a great friend and counselor.

Brad Kuhlman started on our show as a production assistant, which is a fancy title for a gopher. He began working for us before our second show, so Brad has seen a lot of changes over the years. He was so good at fetching coffee, he was promoted to associate producer after just two weeks on the job. He really has a talent for producing very tight and extremely entertaining shows.

Brad Kuhlman,
PRODUCER 1991–1996

I recall a great story about a show that actually never aired. We were still fighting a few battles to break out of the typical talk show mode and set a new standard for television, albeit a substandard. Anyway, there was only so much we could get away with because Multimedia was an extremely conservative company.

I wanted to do an entire show from a hot tub. I found a very

This is a show from our '95 season. I'll bet that outfit makes a lot of noise in the dryer.

big-busted X-rated dancer, who also was a swinger, to be one of our guests. She was wearing a teeny bikini that had these two little strings that wrapped around her neck and came to a little V at the bottom. But before she went out there, one of the executives from the company refused to let her go on camera so exposed, which is ridiculous when you see the shows that make it on our air today. So she ended up having to wear a big flannel shirt over her bathing suit. She tied the bottom of the shirt in a bow, and she looked like Mary Ann from *Gilligan's Island!*

So, we start the show, and I'm really excited because I'm thinking, *this* is great television. I'm thinking about the viewers at home seeing this on their sets, a bunch of beautiful women in a hot tub talking about their wild lifestyles! But the show took a

RINGMASTER!

really weird turn when all of a sudden one of the women started to cry because her brother disapproved of her lifestyle. And things just started to unravel from there.

Family members in the audience started in on each other because they were also upset. So now you had all of these depressed strippers sitting fully clothed in a hot tub. The show was going nowhere. It looked awful. It wasn't racy. It just looked stupid. Backstage, the arguing was a show in itself. "Let 'em take off their tops." "No, we'll all be fired."

Finally, the show sunk of its own weight. We didn't remove the tops; we just removed the guests. Jerry left the studio, and one of the producers went out and apologized to the audience for what they'd seen. He explained that *"The Jerry Springer Show"* was a "topical program and a respectable show."

Yeah, right!

One of my favorite shows involved this very eccentric woman named Coco. I never really did get a handle on what her story really was, but one day Richard Dominick handed me a piece of paper with a phone number and a picture of this woman on it and told me to call her. We weren't sure what we were going to do with her, but she clearly belonged on our show. She was just wild and bizarre.

She really wanted to be on the show; so in talking to her the first time, she told me how she liked to change in front of the window while her neighbors watched. It really turned her on. So her first show was called, "Exhibitionists." The audience loved her.

After her first show, she kept calling us up and telling us that she had a huge crush on Jerry. She said she was in love

A transsexual, a punk-rocking granny, a talk show host, and a woman named "Coco." The diversity on our stage makes Ellis Island look like Stepford.

and couldn't stop thinking about him. Apparently, she claimed that every time the show would come on television, she had to touch herself. So we brought her on a second time. That's when she started this whole routine where she'd jump up and down, stomping her feet, and chasing Jerry all around the studio. It was some of the funniest TV you'd ever want to see, because Jerry would literally run away from her. She would say to him, "I want you, Jerry," and just chase him all over.

The thing with Coco was that she turned into a real high-maintenance guest. If the show was supposed to start at nine, she wouldn't show up until 10:30. And there was no pleading with her. She would refuse to answer her phone at the hotel and lock herself in the room until she was ready. She wore these crazy outfits, and had really long fingernails, big hair, and Tammy Faye makeup. I can see how it could take her so long to achieve that "look." But there was nothing we could do, and it got tricky because you have an audience waiting. You've got time restrictions. You have to pay the crew overtime, and it became a real drag. But her shows were always really good, so we always waited her out.

The last time I saw Coco was after a show a few years ago. There's a little bar in the NBC Tower, where we tape the show. I was down there after the taping with my then girlfriend Sarah, who at the time was also working on the show. Coco claimed to be psychic, and she did this whole reading on Sarah and me that day. She said that we were going to be together forever and that she saw music being a part of our lives, probably in work. Well, today Sarah is my fiancée and is now the director of development for MTV. Maybe we should have had Coco on one of our psychic shows. . . .

Other shows I get asked about a lot are the Tweaky Dave shows. Tweaky Dave was a homeless teenager who lived in Hollywood. Richard Dominick had gotten hooked up with this guy, Neil, who ran an organization in LA called Youth Escaping the Streets.

But there were a lot of problems with Neil because he worked outside of the system. And the system didn't like Neil because of that. He didn't do things the way you're supposed to do them. And he would let kids sleep at his house instead of forcing them to get a job, and he would have them do other things so that they could survive on the street. I really don't know if he was a good guy or a bad guy. It seemed that he was a good guy. The kids raved about him and said, "He takes care of us."

When we needed certain kinds of guests, we used to go to Neil. Neil led us to Tweaky Dave.

Tweaky Dave made his first appearance on our show back in '91, when we were still in Cincinnati. Richard was the producer and I was the associate producer at the time. His real name was Dave Miller, but everybody called him Tweaky Dave or Tweaky because he was a tweaker, and that's a name for a speed freak.

He weighed probably between 85 to 90 pounds, and he had maybe two or three teeth, and they were just black. His cheeks were caved in. He just looked like death on wheels. He was on death's doorway every time you saw him. I remember he used to have a padlock that he wore as an earring. From one show to the next, I remember seeing his ear, and it was like ripped open more and more every time, until it finally gave way to the weight of that padlock.

Anyway, the story with Tweaky was that when he was nine, he ran away from home and moved to the streets of Hollywood, where he'd lived ever since. He used to tell this story about how his father had put a gun to his head and shot him. That's why he said he ran away. He said that on his first day on the streets, he started begging for food and also began prostituting—all at the age of nine. He had this horrific story. He was also dying of leukemia and he had no treatment out in the streets. He was just the most pitiful sight you ever wanted to see. But he was smart and he could talk, and he knew how to talk, and he knew what people wanted to hear.

We could put him on the stage and have Jerry say, "Tell us your story," and he would go on for an hour. And you'd be riveted. That's what we looked for in our guests. He was gold, as Richard would say.

We kept bringing him back because every time we put him

on, people responded. They would send checks in the mail to the show. We'd have checks made out to Tweaky Dave. I think some woman even sent cash! It was unbelievable. They were $10, $15, $25 checks. It wasn't anything big, but people felt they could help this kid out. We either sent them back or tried to forward what we could to Tweaky, but remember that he lived on the street so he wasn't easy to find nor do I think he had a bank account to cash the checks.

We actually got a lot of offers from people to take him in and give him a life. So we made that happen, which, unfortunately, didn't work out. He went to live with somebody for a few months, and he ended up running away and living back on the streets because that's really where he wanted to be. He didn't want to be living under somebody else's rules.

In a related show, and it's one of the best shows I ever did, was when we shot Tweaky on location in Hollywood. It was like a documentary on what Tweaky's life was like. He showed us where he ate out of Dumpsters, and we taped him going through garbage cans. He even took us to meet some of his friends out in the street where we went to a squat, which is just an abandoned house where 25 to 30 homeless kids live—until the cops chase them.

I heard that Tweaky Dave recently died—apparently of hepatitis.

I remember Tweaky vividly. He captured everyone's attention on the show.

Here's my "Final Thought" after one of Tweaky Dave's appearances on our show.

Final Thought, Aired July 12, 1994

You know, for too many, the streets are home. It shouldn't be like that . . . and for some . . . if we're looking to point fingers—it's their own fault. Surely, some are strong enough to get their act together—to find work, to find a place to live with a roof and running water. For some, the hand that begs ought to be the hand that works, and if they're looking for a reason for why they are homeless, they only need to find a mirror.

But what about the kids? Kids abandoned or abused . . . with no one to love them, care for them . . . those not raised in Donna Reed–like homes, what do we do about them? It's easy to say, "You're crazy, kid. Go back home." But sometimes that's not possible or even advisable and our institutional remedies are not always much better.

The point is, there is not a blanket answer. Clearly the streets are hell and rarely better than home. But when they are, we have to provide alternatives. Shelters, hot lines, counseling, and recognition that when kids are victims and ignored as such, they will become criminals. Doubters need only to check the headlines.

Some of our most powerful shows are taped on location. Here, I sit down with runaways who live on the streets of Hollywood to discuss the dangers of teen heroin abuse.

I did several more shows on homeless and runaway teenagers. We spent a week on the streets of Hollywood talking with teenagers who'd made the streets their home. It was unforgettable and an eye-opening experience for everyone who worked on, as well as saw, these shows.

Now, you may have heard that we've been under a lot of pressure lately to cut back the fighting on our show, so in an effort to comply with upper management's request, we decided to do a real love story—Jerry Springer style of course. . . .

Melinda Chait,
PRODUCER 1997–PRESENT

I remember finding this story on "the cart," which is where all of the telephone calls that come into the show get routed to. The call to action was, "Do you have a bizarre or unusual lifestyle your family disapproves of?"

This man named Mark Mathews called in and his story was about the woman he loved and was married to. Actually, her name was Pixel. We were soon to find out that this "love of his life," to whom he'd been married for five years, was a pony. We decided to name the show, "I Married a Horse!"

My associate producer, Toby Yoshimura, did the initial interviews with Mark to see if this guy was for real. After a lot of skeptical questioning from Toby, Mark finally offered to send some proof that he lived as man and wife with Pixel.

Give Daddy a kiss.

Mark sent very explicit photographs of himself and Pixel engaging in oral sex and intercourse. Mark explained to Toby the do's and don't's of approaching a sexual encounter with a horse. He explained that "you want to wear shoulder pads and knee pads, and a crash helmet isn't a bad idea either. You'll also need a lot of K-Y jelly because Vaseline doesn't work. You'll either get a flying lesson from the horse or a sexual experience that's unforgettable!"

We couldn't fly Pixel in because we would have had to build a crate for her, which my production budget just didn't allow for, so she came by trailer. And once Mark and Pixel did get to town, he wanted to sleep in the stable where we put Pixel.

The taping was great. We "humanized" Pixel as much as we could by having her come out onstage wearing a bridal veil. They nuzzled and made out in front of the audience, and you could genuinely tell that they were like any other couple in love. In fact, we even did a remote shoot from the house that Mark and Pixel share, where they do indeed sleep in the same bed and live together as any other husband and horse . . . make that wife.

Aside from Mark, we had two other guests who have sex with their dogs, one man and one woman. I wanted to find another kind of animal to round out the show and I did, except that the guy who was having sex with his sheep refused to bring his sheep on the air, and the man who does it with his goat just disappeared.

Although some might refer to this act as "beastiality," those who participate say they'd rather refer to themselves as "Zoos." Mark claims that there are thousands of people who have sexual encounters with animals. They communicate with each other through the Internet. In fact, once a year there is a convention called "ZooFest," where Zoos get together and celebrate their happy unions.

Obviously, this was one of our most outrageous shows— clearly our most controversial. I consider this my "crowning achievement" at *"The Jerry Springer Show,"* because, as requested . . . there wasn't one fight!

Sometimes we get calls from people and their stories sound too good to be true . . . and sometimes they are. But I did a show called "Marriage Confessions" that turned out to be very real, despite my initial doubt. We received separate calls from a husband and wife, who both claimed to be having an affair with the husband's best friend, who was a man. I didn't believe their story at first, but I decided to bring them in for the show anyway.

I called the two men into my office and explained to them that I couldn't go forward with the show because I had some doubt as to whether or not they were telling me the truth. I told them that they didn't look gay to me; and in order for me to give the show a green light, they had to prove that they were involved with each other.

Well, one of the guys gave me some excuse about having just had his tongue pierced and that he couldn't possibly risk kissing anyone for fear of infection. But I insisted that if they didn't somehow prove to me that their story was real, they were off the show. Suddenly the other guy leapt out of his seat, grabbed his lover, and they started just going at it, grabbing each other's butts and everything! It was like watching two construction workers make out.

When they finished, they both commented to each other how hot it was with the two tongue pierces. Now I know good television when I see it, so I suggested that if they wanted the audience to believe them, they should do it again on the air—which they did.

The wife was totally dumbstruck. And then she dropped the bomb on her husband that she was also having an affair with the best friend. The husband got really mad when he heard this because he thought they should have all been in on it together . . . as in threesome!

"Jerry Springer" . . . I get into that.
—HARRY CONNICK JR.
ENTERTAINMENT WEEKLY'S COLUMN CALLED "GUILTY PLEASURES"

Rachelle Consiglio,
SENIOR PRODUCER 1995—PRESENT

I have the dubious honor of having the only guest who was arrested for something he did on our show. It was called, "I'll Never Forgive You!" It featured a husband who was very abusive toward his wife. He never let her out of the house unless he knew exactly where she was going. He never gave her any money.

So he comes on our show and claims that he is a "changed" man and he wants her back. The wife's sister came on the show to confront the husband, and there was definitely bad blood between them. The husband blamed the sister for the problems he was having with his estranged wife. In fact, when she came out, the husband couldn't even sit on the same stage with her, so he got up and left. When the sister finally came backstage after the show, he punched her square in the face and she was knocked to the floor! Security tackled him and put him in what's called a "sleeper hold." The sister bounced right back up and came after him, even though he was still being subdued. As security was dragging him away, the sister started shouting, "Too bad you can't pack a punch!"

The reason this was such a big deal was that, at the time, fights weren't as prevalent as they are now, but we do not tolerate a man hitting a woman on our show—ever. We always ask if she wants to press charges. Usually they don't, but not this time. We took him to the Green Room, where he started to sob uncontrollably. He was trying to apologize, but no one was really listening at that point. In fact, all he accomplished was freaking

This is a father and his stepson fighting over a woman. She happened to be the father's ex-wife and his stepson's fiancée. And you thought your family was strange.

out our next guests who were waiting to go on for their show called "I'm So Fat and I Can't Lose Weight!"

When the police showed up, he was still sobbing, and one of the cops said to him, "You're on national TV. Why don't you act like a man and stop crying?"

It was pretty pathetic.

Todd Schultz is our stage manager. He has a lot of responsibility on the show, but this next story goes above and beyond the call of duty. . . .

Todd Schultz,
STAGE MANAGER/SECURITY 1994–PRESENT

I've seen everything at this show, and the one show I'll never forget was called "I Cut Off My Manhood!" The guest who was on was a guy named Earl Z. Earl was being stalked by a gay guy and actually thought that if he cut off his penis, the guy would stop following him. It wouldn't be my plan, but that's what he did. He cut it off and flushed it down the toilet for the alligators to feast on.

I remember Jerry asking Earl why he didn't change his phone number or move instead of cutting off his penis! I thought Jerry had a point. . . .

As stage manager, I was given the auspicious job of finding out if Earl had any medical photos or other pictures to show the studio audience. But he didn't, so he had to pull down his pants to show me he was telling the truth. It hurts just thinking about it. He still had his testicles and what looked like a large belly button. We took a Polaroid to show the audience, just in case anyone doubted his story. He told me that he could still get aroused and perform sex with what was left. He also told me that he could use urinals, but if he had to aim downward into a toilet it didn't work so well.

Steve Hyrniewicz was our stage manger from 1992 to 1994. He garnered a lot of attention on the show while he was there. He was around for our first fight and a part of the evolution of the show. He recalls some fun memories of his days on *"The Jerry Springer Show."*

Steve Hyrniewicz,
STAGE MANAGER 1993–1997

I made a couple of on-camera appearances when I was working on *"The Jerry Springer Show."* One time, Sheila Rosenbaum was doing a show about strippers and their parents who wanted them to stop. It was sort of a harsh show and one of the groups had dropped out right before the taping. So Sheila asked if I would do a striptease to help lighten up the show and fill up time.

I was a little unsure if I wanted to do it, but in the end I did, and I have to admit, it was great fun. I went up on the stage fully dressed, the tech crew put on some sexy music, and I began. First, I slowly and seductively removed my stage manager headphones and the crowd loved it, so I really started to ham it up. Eventually, everything came off except a pair of cheesy heart boxer shorts I had and my pants remained at my ankles. When

Steve getting pointers for his striptease from Danny the Wonder Pony. . . . Don't ask.

the dance was over, I hopped off the stage and resumed my duties. Where was this paragraph in my job description?

The only other time I was on camera was when we had a show called "Jerry's Favorite Secret Crushes." On this show, I was backstage putting a microphone on a guy to go out onstage to meet a girl who had come on the show to have a dinner with her secret crush. So they start to describe the guy she has the crush on, and to my surprise they weren't talking about the guy next to me at all; they were describing me!

The next thing I knew, I was being called up onstage to have a candle-lit dinner with this girl on the show, and the whole audience was chanting, "Steve, Steve, Steve." Man, did I feel like a dork. Apparently, I wasn't so bad, because after that show I got a ton of fan mail. Too bad I had a girlfriend at the time.

Here's a sampling:

Steve,
Hi! I watched "The Jerry Springer Show" on August 15th and I fell in love with you! I think you are ABSOLUTELY HOT! My name is J-- and I'm an outgoing 15-year-old sophomore who attends J-- High School! Well, since I called "The Jerry Springer Show" and tried getting through seventy-three times, and finally did so I could get the address, what I would like is you to send me a picture of yourself or a letter. You would make my day and I would be satisfied! Thanks.
(Heart)
J--

P.S. Even a postcard from the show will do! I love you!

Jerry,

I am writing this letter as a follow-up to a couple of phone calls I made regarding a special request I have of you.

As I mentioned in my previous message, I would very much like for my daughter to meet Steve, your floor director.

I live with my daughter and watch your show regularly. Her office is here at home, and she instructs me to let her know when Steve is on camera. She constantly tells me she would really like to meet him. My daughter is very special to me and has done a lot for me, so I would like to do something special for her. So if there is a show that relates to this situation, please keep me in mind.

A.C.

A lot of our staff members get fan mail, and they love it. Sometimes it's inevitable that a producer strikes up a relationship with the guests they book. A certain level of trust is built and there is a bond that remains after the show is over. Gina Huerta, one of our producers, has such a story:

Gina Huerta,

PRODUCER 1996–PRESENT

My associate producer, Ryan Sucher, and I get pretty close to some of our guests. It's important to gain their trust so that they will give you the best possible story and not hold back on the air. One group we became close to was for a show called, "I'm Pregnant by My Brother." Follow me here. The girl in the story was seventeen years old when she became pregnant by her half-brother . . . but she dumped him and started going out with the other half-brother. They all had the same mother, but the boys had a different father than the girl. The mother in this story hated her daughter, not because she was sleeping with her half-brothers but because, "She's a slut."

Needless to say, there was a lot of fighting on the show between the parents and the kids, so the kids looked to us as their friends, which we were. What I didn't realize was how much they had become attached to us during our week or so together. When the baby was finally born, they asked Ryan and I to be the child's godparents! As much as we would have liked to help this child and guide her moral life (which might need some tending to), we had to refuse. We thought doing that would be crossing the line of professionalism.

Brenda You is our assistant director. She has been involved with some of our more controversial shows, such as Klan-related shows, when she worked as a producer. Here she recalls some great stories on shows that cross the line—even for us.

Brenda You,

ASSISTANT DIRECTOR 1994–PRESENT

Jerry is a fairly easygoing guy when it comes to doing our show, but he doesn't always allow producers to get everything they might want. Firstoff, he will not do a show that involves people who deny that the Holocaust happened. Jerry is also hesitant in doing shows with pregnant women who might get violent. He allows them to do their stories, but there is tightened security to ensure that they don't fight onstage because it would endanger that unborn child who did not consent to being on the show. When they do fight, Jerry immediately ends that segment and takes them off the stage.

Jerry has ended a few other shows because either he did not believe their story was true or he believed that what was being said was not proper, even for our show. One like this was called "My Boyfriend Is a Pimp." He said to the participants on the stage that he did not believe their story and ended the show. The audience booed them onstage, but Jerry gave everyone in the audience rain checks to come back another time.

This show made the papers as being another "fake show" on *"The Jerry Springer Show."* Of course the only thing they omitted from the story was the fact that Jerry ended the show and called them on their act.

The only time I can think that Jerry ended a show against the will of the producers was a show called, "I'll Make You a Porn Star." In this show there was a man onstage who claimed he could make anyone a porn star. It was a decent show up until the man claimed he could do it with 13- and 14-year-old children as well. With this, Jerry literally walked off the set and refused to

continue the show. The show was never edited or aired. Jerry drew the line and he stood by it.

One of the most unusual shows I ever was witness to was a show where we had two sets of love triangles. The first segment went off without a hitch. The usual stuff went down, two angry women, one two-timing man. When the next segment started, the first woman came out and attacked one of the women who was already onstage. I didn't know what she was doing. It was like she didn't even know who was her man's mistress because she was still backstage and she was attacking the guests in another unrelated story.

As it turned out, the night before the show, the man in the second segment who was two-timing on the women he had come with found his way into the other triangle's story and ended up sleeping with one of those women! So the two-timing man in the second segment was now three-timing with another woman who was in the segment before his. Some people really cannot keep it in their pants.

Did you get all of that? Sometimes these love triangles are more like octagons. . . .

It's difficult for me to talk about "The Jerry Springer Show." Everything I haven't blocked out, I'd have to reen-act with dolls.

—JOHN HENSON
HOST, TALK SOUP E! ENTERTAINMENT TELEVISION

TEN
The Fights

I think the most frequently asked question I receive is about the fighting on *"The Jerry Springer Show."* Everyone wants to know if the fights are fake or real. Being that I'm the least confrontational guy in the world, I never stick around long enough to actually watch any of the fights. With a nose like mine, I figure I'm an easy target, so I hustle out of the studio or at least hover in an obscure corner until it's over. Hey, I'm no Geraldo. The truth is, when it comes to physical confrontation, I'm pretty much of a wimp.

That's why we have a staff of security professionals who oversee and protect the needs of our guests and audience members. And while the media would like you to believe that

Jay Leno and I found out what happens when you ask my security guys to smile. It ain't pretty, is it?

the violence is, in fact, staged, I can honestly tell you that it is not. Richard Dominick, in an effort to answer this omnipresent question, issued an invitation to any member of the media to come work security on our show for just one day. It is no surprise that not one single journalist, reporter, critic, or other member of the media accepted his invitation.

Now, how come there's been so much fighting on our show? There are several reasons for that. Understand, there was no initial intent to have fighting. Indeed, we never used to have it. But one day we had the Klan on, and things got out of hand—

and suddenly, there's a fight. I thought we were done. I figured that would be our last show. I was wrong.

What we saw was that our best shows—those that were most compelling—those that enticed the viewer to freeze the remote—were those where there was real personal conflict, real issues of confrontation. That didn't necessarily mean fighting, but it did mean showing real people honestly responding to something they felt deeply about at the moment. Normally, when a fight did result (when I say "fight," it rarely was anything more than cursing or shouting, wrestling, and maybe some hair pulling——certainly not acceptable behavior, but, nonetheless, real), we would edit it out of the show so the viewer at home wouldn't see it. But when Universal bought the show, they said, "If it happens, show it. Viewers are entitled to see life as it is, even if it isn't always pretty. The show is what it is."

Well, you know the rest of that story. When we started to show our show unedited and unsanitized, it was as if the American public was getting a look at a slice of contemporary life that heretofore had never been seen on television. Viewership went through the roof. For the first time in ten years, *Oprah* was surpassed as the number-one talk show in America. Suddenly, everybody was talking *Jerry*. That is, everyone except the guests. They weren't talkin'; they were fighting.

So there I was, a guy of absolutely no talent and no training in this field, suddenly sitting on top of the world, all because I had guests who fight. It didn't make any sense. Believe me, anyone could do my show, and most—a hell of a lot better than me.

Anyway, back to the fighting.

You should know that I've never been in a fight in my life. I'm either a wimp or a pacifist. I don't believe violence is ever the answer, except in self-defense. Then how do I explain my show and violence on television, in general?

As I said, but for self-defense, I don't ever think violence is an appropriate response. However, I do think it's important for television to reflect real life—the bad as well as the good. But it should never put something on that encourages or entices bad or violent behavior.

That is why the fictional violence we see on prime-time television and in movies, where guys are blowing each other away with AK-47s and Uzis, where we have five killings or muggings or rapes before each commercial break, is the kind of violence that is dangerous to our society because it's made to seem glamorous and exciting. Indeed, our biggest movie stars today are the ones who wipe out the most people. This kind of entertainment is dangerous because it's done in a very enticing way, with drop-dead gorgeous actors, beautiful backgrounds and scenery, amazing special effects, and powerful music. It's all put in a very provocative package, so kids, even though they know it's fiction, are encouraged, even subliminally, to

The double hair-pull. Jimmy tries to untangle this classic "Springer Show" maneuver.

fantasize about such behavior. And the more and more we see these kids walking into classrooms with their guns, spraying death and destruction among teachers and classmates alike, the more it should become clear that this form of enticing dramatic fictional entertainment is horribly destructive and dangerous.

On the other hand, there is nothing, I repeat, nothing at all enticing or attractive about the behavior you see on my show, nothing that ever says to the viewer of whatever age, "Gee, this is a productive or exciting or attractive way to behave." Indeed, nobody ever could watch our show and say, "Wow, I think tomorrow I'll become a transsexual who sleeps with a horse!"

The point being, if those in the industry are serious about eliminating violence on television and in the movies, the kind of violence that entices viewers to become violent themselves, then fine. Eliminate the programming that shows guns, and knives, and drugs, and killings, the kind of fictional programming that makes it seem so exciting.

Look, as crazy as our show is, we don't ever show guns, or knives, or killings, or rapes. Indeed, we don't ever show violence that in any way is enticing to anybody. Can the rest of television say that? Of course not. It feeds on violence. And the best response critics can come up with is to start arguing about a silly talk show. You can see how it's hard to take their protestations and hand-wringing seriously. Don't we have bigger issues to talk about?

Now that I've said my piece, I know you still want to know about the action on our show.

Steve Wilkos, the head of our security staff, has become a pop icon himself these days. He gets asked for his autograph as often as I do whenever we're out together. Guys are always coming up to him and saying, "Hey, Steve, put me in a head-lock." Girls just want to rub his head. Anyway, Steve has really been through it all on our show. Imagine a job where you know you're going to have to step into the ring and get pushed around at least a dozen times a day. We probably don't pay him or any of his security staff enough for what they do!

Since I am never around during the fights, the guys who are in the ring are in the best position to give you the inside track on all the action. Ask any of them if the fights are fake and they'll show you their war wounds.

Steve Wilkos,

HEAD OF SECURITY 1993–PRESENT

I've seen a lot of fights on *"The Jerry Springer Show."* As the head of security, I really have to prepare myself for the job. You have to be in relatively good shape because you're going to have to wrestle up there five, six times a day at least. I've been injured in every possible way you can imagine. I've been poked in the eyes and lost my contacts, I've snapped my groin, I had a woman get her entire mouth around my elbow and bite down, I've been kicked, punched, shoved, and even thrown off the stage by a couple of wrestlers. That proved to be the toughest fight I ever had to break up on the show. Most people who come on the show don't really know how to fight, but these guys knew what they were doing. They were little guys too, but they had the moves. They knew how to get out of our holds easily, and they really wanted to go at it with each other. So as I'm pulling this guy back off the other guy, I guess he used my own weight against me and the next thing I knew, I was off the stage and on my back. That was embarrassing. Actually, it's kind of funny, but smaller guys whose wives are cheating on them like to come on the show so they can get a couple of licks in on the other guy and they know they're not going to get hurt because we're there to keep everyone from getting hurt. Then all their friends at home think he's a stud because he kicked some ass on TV.

Usually when a guest hits me or any one of my guys onstage, they apologize afterward or during the commercial break. They just get so pumped up to be on television that they lose control. One time, Jimmy Sherlock and myself were breaking up this fight between two women, and I felt bad about it but

Any of my security guys will tell you: the worst fights are between women. Here Steve and Dan have their hands full preventing a catfight.

it was just so funny at the time. My girl kicked Jimmy right in the groin, and as he began to buckle over in pain, his girl turned around and punched him in the face. I just broke up laughing. They did say they were sorry.

I often travel with Jerry when he makes an appearance and work as his personal security. We were down in Jamaica doing MTV's *Springer Break.* It was a total mob scene wherever we went. While we were there, we did a mock *"Jerry Springer Show."* It was set up just like the real show.

The show was about roommates. One roommate was sleeping with his roommate's girlfriend. Typical Springer stuff. Of course it broke out into a fight. After the show, the guests went to the papers and said that they had been prompted into fighting and *"The Jerry Springer Show"* was once again in the papers for having "set up" fights, but the Springer staff had nothing to do with the fights, other than breaking them up.

I think the media has been very unfair to Jerry and the show. First of all, the fights are real. These people get up there with some serious problems being presented to them, and with the added adrenaline of being on national TV they just go berserk. Most of the news programs that criticize the show are doing it because Jerry is number one now and to include Jerry's show in their own story just helps their own ratings in the end.

This poor guy thought he was dating a woman. When he learned that she was a man, he tried to get one good shot in before Steve could pull him off.

Todd Schultz,
STAGE MANAGER/SECURITY 1994–PRESENT

For some reason, I still get involved in breaking up all the fights, and I'll tell you, one thing I've learned from this show, NEVER CROSS A WOMAN. Men have egos and will stop fighting if they think they're going to lose, but women, they don't care if they win or lose, they just want to do as much damage to whoever they can in the amount of time they're given. We're up there to restrain people from fighting and getting hurt. Once you get ahold of them, the guys back off. But women, forget about it.

You only hurt the ones you love. I'm sure Steve thanked Jimmy for his support on this one.

They bite you, kick you in the shins, pull back your fingers, anything to get in another shot.

The toughest fighters to restrain are the transsexuals, who fight like women but have the strength of men. One time these two women were going at it, fighting, pulling hair, throwing their spiked heels, the works, and this one girl is going so crazy she didn't realize that she was pulling her own hair. I said to her, "Stop pulling hair." And she said to me, "I'm not pulling hair; she is!" And I said, "No, you don't understand. You're pulling your own hair." She didn't even care. She stopped for a moment and charged the other woman again a minute later.

Jimmy Sherlock,
SECURITY 1996–PRESENT

I've seen a lot of fights up there, and there is no way they're fake. Most of us up there are like 6'2", 230 pounds, and can take care of ourselves. I'd like to see one of our media critics get up there and try and break the fights up.

The biggest fight I was ever a part of had to be the Klan vs. the JDL, the Jewish Defense League. The Klan had seven people onstage and the JDL came out with another seven or so and had a bunch of supporters in the audience, too. As the JDL took the stage, one of the Klan members took off his hood and had a yarmulke on. The leader of the JDL, who was an older guy, tried to take it off his head and the fight broke out. Luckily we had a full staff of six guys, all off-duty Chicago policemen and a seventh security guy who was sitting in the "hot seat" in the audience. (The hot seat is where we put a security guy in the audience, close to the stage, just in case anything happens . . . like this fight. No one except our staff knows he's there.)

So everyone onstage is starting to throw blows and chairs at each other, and we rushed the stage to get it under control, which was no easy task. To make matters worse, the supporters of the JDL who were in the audience rushed the stage as well. So we've got 20 people onstage fighting and there are only seven of us up there to break it up. Luckily, the audience members who rushed the stage backed down pretty quickly, but different fights kept breaking out, and this went on for at least 15 minutes. Now a fight that lasts for three minutes is a long fight, so you can imagine what this was like.

Security usually doesn't see the guests before they're up onstage, but when it's a big Klan show or another militant-type show we go back to the Green Room and introduce ourselves as Chicago police officers and tell them that we are not going to hurt them and that they are not going to hurt us or anybody else for that matter. And if we tell them to calm down and they don't calm down there is the possibility that they are going to be arrested. So far, in the two and a half years I've been around, no one has been arrested though.

I do remember a sort of funny fight. It involved a guest named Reno. Now Reno is a woman who lives her life as a man. She's a very nice guest and we've had her on the show a bunch of times. Reno's girlfriend, Monique, who was onstage with her, is really hot. Another guest onstage confronted Reno and said to Monique that she should be with a "real" man, like him. With this, Reno, standing 5'5", 135 pounds, goes flying at this guy and starts to really brawl.

So I darted up there to break it up, and Reno's "manhood" slipped out of the bottom of her pants. I guess she wears this thing all the time. So as I'm pulling her apart from this guy, I whisper into her ear, "Hey, Reno, your manhood just fell out." This DID end the fight and Reno sat back down and secured it back into place. I don't think this made it on the air.

ELEVEN
The Rise of Jerry Springer

The 1997–98 season will, no doubt, be remembered as Jerry Springer's year. It . . . is the fastest growing show in syndication ever. This is a show that has taken independent stations from worst to first in many markets.

—MARC BERMAN
SELTEL, A TELEVISION RESEARCH FIRM

In early 1997, Universal was determined to raise our ratings to attract more advertisers to our show. In an effort to do so, Ned Nalle, the president of Universal Worldwide Television Production, gave Richard Dominick the green light to go for it and push the limits as far as we could. This decision by Jim Mac-Namara and Ned Nalle empowered us to succeed. Basically, they told us to save our best shows for sweeps. They loosened the reins on us editorially and allowed us to air the shows we had been shooting as they were. What culminated was a buildup of energy that took us from a 2.8 rating to a 9 one year later, and being the first talk show ever to surpass Oprah in the ratings.

In the spring of 1997, *"The Jerry Springer Show"* started

making a dramatic climb in both ratings and popularity. We were finally airing shows much closer to the way they were shot and not editing out as much of the action. The viewers started taking notice of the outrageousness, and the stations started noticing a sharp rise in viewership. One reason I think the dramatic rise was happening is directly related to a brilliant idea brought to us by Real Entertainment. They are the production company that released the tremendously successful *Cops* videotape series through a massive direct response marketing campaign. It was a huge success for them, and they were absolutely certain they could do the same thing with *"The Jerry Springer Show."* I, of course, had my doubts, not in their ability to sell, but in my own rising popularity. Scott Barbour, the owner of Real Entertainment, explains his idea like this:

I wish I could take sole credit for creating the idea to release the "Too Hot for TV" videotape series, but it was really a great meeting of the minds. We had already successfully released a series of videotapes based around outtakes for the television show *Cops,* and we needed to find another vehicle to follow up with on the heels of that success. We wanted to find somebody who was on a roll and was like a lightning rod to attract the kind of attention we wanted to garner.

Greg Meidel, who was the chairman of Universal television at the time, and Louis Feola, the president of Universal video, had already come up with the idea independently at the time my company had approached them about doing something with Jerry. We all agreed that *"Jerry Springer"* was an underexploited property. It had garnered some attention over the four years it had been on the air, but the upside potential had yet to be tapped. We wanted to build a brand around the show in order to

It ain't all glamour. Here, I shamelessly promote Jerry Springer merchandise.

heighten the attention and its recognition. Within Universal, there was some hesitancy because the content of the videos was going to be racy, to say the least.

So, in true Hollywood fashion, we were in the right place at the right time. We edited together the first "Too Hot for TV" video and released it through direct response ads on television. We reached an impressive level of success, which then allowed us to keep building the line of merchandise and create a catalogue of other items. The line started with around six items in it, and today, less than a year later, there're around sixty items to choose from.

You can now buy hats, T-shirts, key chains, coffee mugs, license plate holders, jackets, sweatshirts, and even boxing gloves called "sock-m-bop-m's" with Jerry's name and/or likeness on it.

Jerry has become a hero for the working class. People believe in the show and enjoy the show. Everyone likes Jerry. There's a sense from his fans that Jerry is their buddy. He's your favorite uncle. When you go out with Jerry everyone wants to meet him, touch him, shake his hand, take a picture with him. And that's all part of why the show has become so successful and enormously popular.

We used television as our key method in offering the *"Jerry Springer"* items. At our peak, we spent millions of dollars on advertising, running 6000 commercials a week. With that kind of exposure, people began to take notice of this man named Jerry Springer. I think people really started to wonder what his show was all about, so they started tuning in, just to see for themselves what all of the hoopla was.

The residual effect for the show was an expanded demographic. The more people were exposed to the commercials for the videotapes, the more curious people got and started to tune in.

We never expected the success we received, but we knew we had a chance at hitting on something big. Once the curve started swinging upward, the show seemed to get a little edgier. It became a little more of an in-your-face kind of show. The commercials we were running allowed the show to mirror the image we were putting out there on their behalf.

Richard Dominick, the executive producer of the show, has been instrumental in allowing us access to find those 30-second clips and tie them together to create uncensored, uninhibited programming. He has such a great feel for the show, and he has been indispensable to us in creating the videos.

To date, we have sold around 2 million copies of the video-tapes, and our web site, GETJERRY.COM, keeps growing in popularity. We have over one million customers exclusively buying *"Jerry Springer"* merchandise. It has become a multimillion-dollar corporation in itself.

The bottom line is this: I believe that Jerry Springer is a national treasure and definitely a national icon. Being a fan of Jerry's is like belonging to a fraternity. I like to tell people that more people watch *"Jerry Springer"* every day than have gone to see *Titanic*. That's when you have to realize just how big he has become.

Yeah . . . right. Who is he talking about anyway?

But do my critics agree that what I'm doing is so important? I don't think so. Most think it's the worst show on television. It's certainly the craziest, silliest, and sometimes stupidest show on television. But is it the worst? I don't know. What I do know is more people watch us during the week than any other show. There must be something the public likes. Can 25 million Americans be wrong? Okay, maybe sometimes.

Look, anyone who hasn't been living under a rock in the last year knows this *rise* hasn't been an easy one. We've come under a great deal of media criticism and scrutiny. Whatever happened to rooting for the underdog anyway?

But, however you view our show, you should know that it seems the more media attention we get, good or bad, the higher our ratings soar. We've had religious groups picket our studio, threatening to boycott the station if they didn't drop our show. There are petitions being circulated by a group called Citizens for Community Values, which sponsors a national campaign to get us off the air. Six thousand signatures from Cincinnati viewers protesting our show . . . and I'm from there!

And who could forget the Carol Marin debacle in the spring of 1997?

One morning in early 1997, Lyle Banks, general manager at WMAQ in Chicago (we use their studio to tape our show), stepped into the elevator I was on and, after the normal pleasantries, picked up on a casual conversation we had had several weeks earlier when we found ourselves sitting next to each other at a dinner during a television programming convention in New Orleans.

"Jerry," he asked, "would you consider doing commentary on our local news?"

Since I had written and delivered nightly commentaries for

NEW YORK POST

LATE CITY FINAL

THURSDAY, APRIL 23, 1998 / Rain developing, 60 / Weather: Page 28 ★★   http://www.nypostonline.com/   · · **50**

THE TRUTH ABOUT JERRY SPRINGER'S SHOW

IT'S A FAKE!

Report: TV's hottest talk show stages phony fights

Guests claim that fights were scripted on the popular show hosted by Jerry Springer (bottom).

DETAILS ON PAGE 3

sixteen years on the news in Cincinnati (six years on radio, ten years on television and won a host of Emmys for them), the suggestion didn't seem particularly out of the ordinary. "Thanks," I said, "but I don't really have time considering my obligations with the show."

"Well, maybe we can work something out, like once a week," was his response, and in that innocence of a conversation—a reasonable request and a reasonable response—an absurd yet much publicized media flap was born. (The media loves to cover itself.)

Understand, I hadn't done anything wrong here. The general manager simply asked me to do something which I admittedly was qualified to do; and even though no salary would be involved, I enjoy writing, so it'd be fun—and only once a week or so—why wouldn't I say yes? It seemed like a no-brainer. The GM asks; you do it.

Well—

On May 5, 1997, I gave my first commentary on the 10:00 news. On May 6, 1997, I gave my last commentary on the 10:00 news.

Carol Marin, the local anchor, had just quit a few days earlier, telling everyone she wouldn't do a newscast of which I was a part. After all, I was the poster child for what was worst about television. The newsroom went crazy. The media went crazy. She was the hero—or at least a martyr—and I was the heavy. Two days later, I was gone—at least from the news set (I still had my show, of course).

It's a great story—certainly a made-for-TV movie. The only problem is—it's not the whole story. You see, what I didn't know at the time was that some people in the higher echelons of the news department and of the station itself, weren't too happy with the newscast. Not the least of their concerns was the fact that their newscasts constantly ran number two in viewership, even though their NBC prime-time programming was a solid number one. In a major market, the local news is expected to keep that huge audience, but in Chicago, for whatever reason, people preferred to get their news from the local ABC affiliate rather than from Carol and Ron (Ron Majors, her coanchor).

Also, Carol and Ron had ongoing differences of opinion with station management over the direction the newscast should be taking. Into this "newsroom in turmoil," I was invited—becoming, in the process, either "the last straw" or a convenient whipping boy, depending on your point of view. Now, over a year and a half later, two questions continue to puzzle me. First, if WMAQ really wanted Carol to stay on, why didn't they just keep her and withdraw their request to me to do a once-a-week commentary when the issue first came up? Surely no station in the world is going to give up their lead anchor for a two-minute weekly guest spot—unless, of course, they want her out in the first place.

And second, if I really was the reason she finally quit—I only stayed there two days. Why didn't she come back *then*? Perhaps the reason which the media—for whatever reason—chose to ignore, was that her leaving had nothing to do with me. The press just jumped on it. It made for great headlines; and sadly, as we're seeing more and more these days—with reporters admitting they make up stories, with networks and newspapers having to issue full-page and front-page apologies under threat of lawsuit—journalism bows to one master alone—**HEADLINES**. Too often, truth is only a coincidental by-product.

RINGMASTER!   **211**

Now while I'm on the subject—I have a further question about the whole matter. If she was going to have a problem with me doing a two-minute commentary once a week, why didn't she ever come to me about it before grandstanding with her "If I don't get my way, I quit," protestations? After all, we both worked in the same building. It would have been very easy for her to treat this situation in a grown-up and respectful way.

My behavior wasn't above reproach either. I said in an interview that her arrogance was unsettling, that lots of people would be happy to be paid a million dollars a year for reading a prompter. The statement is true, but it wasn't necessary for me to belittle her. I'm sorry I said that.

Anyway, back to the main issue of her allegedly quitting over my commentary. I dwell on it because there is a beautiful irony here. On the surface it appears to be a story about standing up for the integrity of news. In reality, it demonstrated the blatant corruption of that concept.

My first night's commentary dealt with my response to Carol quitting. Remember, at that time the public was led to believe that she was quitting over me. She didn't want me on the same set with her. So I responded that the airwaves don't belong to any one anchor. That her reading off the TelePrompTer didn't give her any right to say or decide who else shall be permitted to address viewers. She was becoming consumed by her own self-importance. She wouldn't be the first anchor to suffer that conceit. Anyway, I made reference to an incident that had occurred while I was mayor of Cincinnati. The neo-Nazis had applied for a permit to march downtown. Normally the permit would have been routinely issued. After all, this is America, and even the despicable are entitled to free speech. But Bill Donaldson, the city manager, along with Henry Sandman, the safety director, came into my office sensitive to my family's personal history (specifically that Mom and Dad had fled the Holocaust and that both my grandmothers and my dad's brother had been exterminated in the camps).

"What should we do about the permit?" they asked.

Mike Ford, who was chief of staff of the mayor's office, was also present at the meeting. Donaldson was clear about it. "It's your call," he said. "If you say so, we'll deny the permit—and fight it in court." I said, "I don't see how we can deny them the right to march, but let me talk to my folks. If it's too hard for them to have their son preside over a city where the Nazis can march, I'll step down and the next mayor can do it." As I explained in my commentary, it was the longest conversation Dad and I ever had about the Holocaust and his feelings about it. But he said, "This is America. It's the freedom this country guarantees even to pigs like them that ultimately protects us all . . . so, sign the permit."

I related this story in my commentary to make the point that if my dad could understand why Nazis must be permitted to march in America, this anchorwoman should be able to understand why someone whose views might well be more liberal than hers should also have a right to expression in this country, even on television. "Too bad she never met my dad," I said.

Now here's how the media distorts truth. A reporter in Cincinnati, Sharon Maloney, writing for the *Cincinnati Post*, figures here's a way to get on the bandwagon. Rather than dealing with the main issue at hand, she grabs on to my dad's line, "Sign the permit." She said I exaggerated the point because, as mayor, it wasn't my signature that went on the permit. No, it wasn't. It was the safety director's signature that did, as if that made a difference in the story. But clearly—unequivocally as Mike Ford, who was at the meeting, attests to—it was purely *my* decision in that instance as to whether or not the permit would be signed. As the city manager said at the meeting in my office, "Jerry, it's your call."

So first, Sharon Maloney was nitpicking just to get a story.

Two, she was wrong. *Dead wrong.*

Three, neither she nor her paper ever apologized or interviewed Mike Ford or publicly admitted that they'd blown it and weren't telling the truth.

She implied—in fact, strongly stated—that it wasn't my decision as to whether that parade permit would be issued to the Nazis, I suspect, hoping to challenge my credibility to be a commentator.

In fact, it was my decision in that case—totally my decision—but there's no obligation and, apparently, often not even much of an effort in the media to get the facts right.

This is admittedly a tiny, inconsequential story, but we all need to know that the media plays with people's lives and reputations every day. They sometimes get it right; but we cannot assume that just because they say it or write it, it's the truth. With apologies to Walter Cronkite, who used to end every broadcast with his signature assurance—"And that's the way it is . . . "—he was wrong. It's not the way it is. Rather, it's the way one reporter, in one location, in one instant of time, happens to see it. Even if they're being honest, they're not necessarily telling the truth. What I mean is, maybe they're not lying, but often they're not smart enough to ask the right questions or maybe the person they're interviewing doesn't have it right or maybe they can't get around their own bias.

Look. Read the paper. Watch the news. Take it all in. But

know it's only an opinion; it's only an individual perspective. It isn't truth.

A final thought on this Carol Marin debacle. Ironically, on the basic issue, Carol and I agreed. I, too, believe there is no room for the tabloidization of news. Indeed, cross-dressing strippers and their attendant love problems do not belong as the subject of a news broadcast. But I never intended to do commentaries on those subjects anyway. I was going to do commentaries on straight news stories, something I had done for ten years (and I hope you'll pardon the immodesty here), something for which I had received countless awards, and nobody was seriously arguing that I wasn't qualified to do that. Somehow that point was lost in the entire furor.

Whatever, life moves on. Though Carol's had some bumps in the road (she had stints on CBS's *Public Eye*, which just got cancelled), she does do reports on one of the local stations here in Chicago—and I'm sure she'll ultimately end up on her feet. The truth is, she can do a good job, and I hope that she gets the chance. It never ever was my idea that she should be let go.

As to what's happened to me, well, since all that, our show just went through the roof, becoming the number-one talk show in America by a large margin. I've been incredibly lucky. Perhaps not surprisingly, the high ratings have also brought more acceptance. A year ago everyone thought what we did was awful. Now, it's fashionable. We get almost nightly mentions on *Letterman* and *Leno*. I've been lucky enough to appear on those shows as well as on *Conan O'Brien, Rosie O'Donnell, The Late Late Show with Tom Snyder, Larry King, Politically Incorrect,* and all of the news programs. I've also had my shot at "acting" on various sitcoms and drama shows, such as *Roseanne, Mar-*

ried . . . with Children, The X-Files, Night Stand, The Steve Harvey Show, The Wayans Brothers, and Between Brothers. The show has been talked about on Chicago Hope, ER, Ellen, Murphy Brown, and now—coming to a theater near you—Ringmaster!—the Movie.

Eric Olson,
ON-AIR PROMOTIONS 1996–PRESENT

Jerry's popularity has affected my marriage. My wife works for *Oprah,* and in the early days, a few years ago, I used to have this great out whenever we were at a wedding or a dinner and we were seated with boring people or people we didn't really know. All I ever had to say was, "You know, Kelly works for the Oprah Winfrey show," and next thing I know she's got to work the room and I was free to head to the bar. But, with Jerry's popularity being what it is today, all anybody ever wants to talk about is *"The Jerry Springer Show."* Now Kelly does to me what I used to do to her. . . .

Face it. Like it or not, *"The Jerry Springer Show"* is like a social cartoon depicting real life in the real world. Of course, some of my critics argue that the show is more like a social disease, but I disagree. In the end, our show will have been a blip on the screen of cultural phenomenon, perhaps remembered in years to come, perhaps not. We're a totally different type of show than Oprah. We're just a wild, silly, outrageous, momentary distraction. We're never going to save humanity—nor will we destroy it.

In a final scene from my upcoming movie, I answer an audience member who ridicules me throughout a taping until I can no longer take any more of his taunting accusations and brutal judgment. (Hey—here's a first—a movie clip in a book!)

The camera is set to film Jerry Springer's point of view as he prepares for his "Dr. Talk" number in the film.

From the upcoming film Ringmaster!—the Movie

Let me tell you something. The rich and famous go on television every single day, hawking their blockbuster, tell-all books—revealing in the process the most intimate and lurid details of their private lives—who they've been sleeping with, what drugs they've been using, a veritable litany of their misdeeds and dysfunctions.

And because they're celebrities, we can't get enough of it. Indeed, nobody ever tells them they can't go on television talking about these things. We just love it.

But when my guests come on television, talking about the exact same issues—just because they're not rich or powerful or famous or because they don't speak the King's English, or wear designer clothes or live in your fancy white suburbs, all of a sudden, what? They're the scum of the earth? How dare they go on television?

Well, here's a program note for you, buddy. This is a slice of American pie. . . . And if you don't like it, bite something else. I would rather spend a month in their trailer than an evening at your elitist country club.

Because at least these people are straight about who they are and what they're thinking. They don't put on airs. They're not hypocrites, they're real. And if, from time to time, they make misjudgments in their personal lives, well, welcome to the human race.

If you don't like what you've seen in my studio today—then get the hell out. But I got news for you. Life's no different out there. You guys just hide it better.

Oh, by the way, take care of yourself. And each other.

Jerry signs an autograph for a guest, "Angel" (played by Jaime Pressly), on his show.

Micki.

TWELVE
Micki & Katie

Her name is Micki. She is better than I deserved. Always has been. It was a blind date. Here's how it happened.

The husband of a young lady I used to date (I always seem to inspire women to marry someone else) called me a few weeks after I arrived in Cincinnati to start practicing law. This was August of '69. He asked me if I was seeing anyone. I told him no, so he fixed me up with his secretary. I picked her up in my new car—a Fiat convertible, top down. We're driving to dinner. Ten minutes into the ride she turns to me as we're speeding down the expressway and throws up all over me.

Okay, I'm certainly no hunk—never been anybody women would drool over—but ten minutes in, do I deserve to be wearing someone's lunch? The young lady obviously felt horrible, humiliated as well as having a bad stomach. I felt terrible for her. I said, "This is silly, why don't I take you home?" I did. We didn't kiss good night. Neither of us felt very attractive at the moment.

The next Friday afternoon, I received another call at the office; it's the same guy. He says, "Jerry?"

I said, "Yes?"

He said, "Jerry, it's Lee. Don't hang up. I've got another one for you to meet."

"How's she feeling?" I asked.

I picked her up that evening. It was Micki. She opened the door and I saw the woman I would love and will love until the day I die.

Four years later we got married. On the surface she was everything I wasn't: Protestant, rural, shy. I was Jewish, European urban, addicted apparently to the spotlight (the light goes on when I open the refrigerator door, which I do every ten minutes). She grew up on a small farm in Kentucky, the product of a wonderful, incredibly close-knit rural family. I had lived my life in London, New York, New Orleans, Chicago. The only horse I had ridden required a quarter every minute and a half.

Her values came from the land: honest, hard-working, totally unpretentious, beautiful on the inside and out, totally dedicated to our daughter, Katie. Simply put, the best woman I've ever known.

The truth is, we've always had a wonderful, caring relationship. But I wasn't always a very good husband to her. In my otherwise wonderful life, it's my one regret. She deserved better.

Surely the highlight in both our lives was the birth of our daughter, Katie. If you're a parent, you know what I'm talking about. You love your kid so much, it blinds you to everything else. I mean, I sometimes have difficulty talking about her without getting choked up. I totally understand now why Mom and Dad loved Evelyn and me so much. It really is inside you. I absolutely believe Katie is an extension of me. Poor kid.

Anyway, in my thirty years in public life, I've always refused to talk about my private life (otherwise, of course, it would no longer be private), but I did once share my thoughts on Katie's birth and what it meant to Micki and me.

I hadn't planned on writing about Micki or Katie, but the words came anyway. And in the end, I realized I wanted to.

Bringing Katie home from the hospital after she was born.

Father's Day Commentary on My Daughter, Katie

She'll be the first Springer eligible to run for the presidency. My sister and I, born in England, and my parents, German-Jewish survivors of the Holocaust, were all constitutionally denied that dream. So here was the first American born of my bloodline. There was no limit to what she'd be. We need only await her birth, which looked for the moment as if it would be a bicentennial one, July 4, 1976.

About to be Cincinnati's mayor, I knew I'd be accused of planning it that way. (What a politician.) But I didn't, and it wasn't to be anyway. Katie was born three days later. Mom, Micki, doing all the work, and me looking on, absorbing life's greatest miracle. She was beautiful. But like a hammer to the heart, something was wrong. The doctors whisked her away to another room. We never had been this way before, so we didn't know. But something didn't seem right, and then we were told they'd have to operate. "Katie has no holes at the back of her nose. She can't breathe if she closes her mouth."

"Welcome to the world, Katie. Pardon the knife—and the drill—and being strapped down in an incubator for five weeks."

It wasn't supposed to be like this. Micki, back and forth to the hospital three times a day, sometimes never leaving, to feed her, hold her, nurture her. I joined in with the holding and nurturing and singing softly, horrible renditions of "K-K-Katie, oh, beautiful Katie . . . " This was a hell of a way to start out a race for the presidency. The news would get worse before it got better. Three months later, "She's legally blind. She's deaf in one ear, partially in the other, balance problems, seizures."

Each visit to the doctor, another blow to the heart. But through God's grace, a mom who gave every moment of her life,

Katie, waiting for the school bus, on her way to an education so that she doesn't have to become a talk show host.

and Katie's determination to beat it all and prove the doctors wrong, she did. Now, entering her senior year in high school, Katie's armed with a great brain, quick wit, kind heart, and her dad's awful sense of humor.

I'm happy to report that Katie sees, hears, and talks unceasingly on the phone with her boyfriend. She's preparing for college and for anything she wants to be. Katie for president. What hurdles couldn't she overcome? She's a gift to all she meets and for me, the greatest Father's Day gift of all.

THIRTEEN
Sports

> **You can always swing the bat again . . .**
> —JERRY SPRINGER

I love baseball. Always have—always will. Before every taping of *"The Jerry Springer Show,"* I meet my producers in Richard Dominick's office for a short briefing, and without fail, I've got a baseball bat in hand. I swing it a few times and, as we break, I take one final turn with the bat and say, "Let's make this the greatest show we've ever done." They look at me as if I'm truly weird—which, of course, I am. But I do love the game.

My office is filled with its memorabilia. Mickey Mantle, Yogi Berra, and Roger Maris adorn my walls. As an adult I've even let non-Yankees slip into my field of worship. I remember meeting Pete Rose when I was Cincinnati's mayor. I was in awe. He's since become a friend. (Of course, he belongs in the Hall of Fame.) And Johnny Bench—what a class act. It's so cool to be able to meet your heroes—regardless of your age.

I met mine a few years ago. It was the greatest week I ever spent alone. I treated myself to the Mickey Mantle–Whitey Ford Dream Camp. You go to Fort Lauderdale in the spring—and for one week, every day you get to play baseball with the

Me in camp around 1959. Don't be impressed, I grounded out to the pitcher.

old-time Yankees. There were 45 guys in the camp and you have to be over 30, and probably because of the expense, most of the guys were in their forties and fifties. The truth is, most of us were probably never good ball players, but in our minds, this was Yankee Stadium and we were now the Yankees.

You get your own uniform, your own locker next to one of the stars—Mantle, Ford, Bill Skowron, Hank Bauer—a litany of Yankee history. You get a baseball card with your own picture and for one week you play a doubleheader with the Yanks every day. You live in the hotel with them, eat every meal with them, and yes, you drink with them. Conscious now of how Mickey died, the writing was clearly already on the wall. We all idolized him, but he was drinking all the time; and you had the feeling that Whitey, who was really running the camp and was Mickey's closest friend there, was the only one trying to keep a handle on him.

Anyway, I remember the final night when we played against the old-timers before a packed house. I was catching, Whitey was on the mound, and out of the dugout here comes Mickey Mantle, getting ready to step into the batter's box. All of a sudden my life is flashing in front of me. This was everything I'd ever wanted. I remember seeing a little boy playing ball in the house, with my mom saying, "Gerald, stop throwing the ball against the wall." I was always pretending to be Yogi Berra or Mickey Mantle. Thinking about this, I started to get teary-eyed. My glasses were fogging up beneath my mask. I was physically shaking as he stepped toward the plate. I was so nervous. Mantle stepping in; Ford on the mound.

All of the sudden I thought to myself, *I'm gonna get hurt.* So, I called a time-out and ran out to the mound. Whitey stares at me in wonderment and, with his thick New York accent, asked, "Whatcha doin?"

"Whitey," I said, "I can't stop shaking."

He put his arm around me like I was in the seventh grade and said, "Get the fuck behind the plate. Mantle hasn't hit in 20 years—and he can't see straight!"

He saw something. He flew deep to left.

Another boyhood hero of mine was Roger Maris, a man who, despite the fact that everyone was against him, just kept stepping up to the plate and hitting home runs. He was the salt of the earth: no flair, no flash, and a no-BS attitude. Of course this has been the fall that his record of 37 years finally fell. While Mark McGwire and Sammy Sosa thrilled the nation with their assault on baseball's most treasured mark, I watched in sadness. Why in sadness? I want to share a commentary I did on Roger Maris while I was an anchor at WLWT in Cincinnati.

Roger Maris Commentary,

AIRED DECEMBER 16–17, 1985

He was my boyhood hero. He dominated the walls of my room with his picture-perfect swing and the summers of my adolescence, as I took on the neighborhood with my self-proclaimed certainties. Maris was the best, I would yell, in a city with lots of alternatives: Mantle, Mays, and DiMaggio among them. He would break Ruth's record, I argued vehemently. Indeed, heroes were uncomplicated then, and Roger was mine.

And now, a quarter of a century later, it still hurts when I hear that my childhood idol, who lived in the shadow of the Babe (or at least of his record), died like him too—of cancer—too young and too painfully.

The death of a man I never knew but loved as a kid brought two thoughts to mind: First, that his assault on the Babe, in that summer of '61, still stands as the most exciting record chase of our lifetime. That's not to say that it will never be broken or that other achievements are less worthy, but understand the moment and what he faced.

You see, America had never had a sports hero like Babe Ruth. Indeed, the Babe made baseball the national pastime—and then became bigger than the sport itself. All legends paled in comparison. Yet Roger Maris, of insignificant note, from a place called Fargo, North Dakota, put on the same uniform as the Babe, in a town already in love with legendary teammate Mickey Mantle, and dared to break the magic "60"—to hit more than 60 home runs in one season. The idea was sacrilege. The media hounded him, fans booed him, and the commissioner of the sport said that the record would have an asterisk because the season was now a little longer.

The nation became obsessed with the chase. Roger Maris, up against a legend and time, each at bat high drama, his hair literally falling out under pressure. And then, on the final day of the season, he did it. Number 61, into the right field seats, and Roger Maris had done what nobody had ever done.

Well, Saturday he did what everybody eventually does: he died.

Which inspired the second thought I had about him this weekend, which is that only childhood offers the purity of vision and heart that invites hero worship. As we now in adulthood hear the obituaries about him, it's comforting to note that nothing we found out about him since suggests that our childhood obsession was misplaced.

Every kid should have a Roger Maris.

Despite my love of sports, I guess I'm not the best advertisement for good health. I mean, I'm lucky. I'm in great health, but I really don't take great care of myself. You see my basic philosophy in life is never run if you can walk. Never walk if you can stand. Never stand if you can sit. Never sit if you can lie down. I mean, it's not as if I haven't joined health clubs in the past. I have. It's just the weights are so heavy. And paying a trainer, when *I'm* the one doing all the work, goes against every grain of my normal monetary stinginess.

I'm thinking of putting out an exercise tape. If you want to be healthy, everything I do, don't. And that's how to be healthy.

I love cheeseburgers. I love fries. I love chocolate malts. But virtually everything I love, I shouldn't have.

Breakfast is really tough. I love eggs, but there's that cho-

Modesty be damned, I love this country.

lesterol thing. Turkey bacon has fat; ditto home-fried potatoes. Coffee has caffeine, decaf has acid, as does juice. Don't put sugar on cereal. NutraSweet kills mice—or something like that. So I'm down to All-Bran cereal, skim milk, dry toast, and Metamucil. This is what I'm supposed to have after I run two miles at six in the morning. And you think people on my show are crazy?

And gone are the soft drinks we grew up with. Now it's drinks that are sugar-free, caffeine-free, calorie-free. Everything's free—but the cost. The can's empty.

And everyone's got these books that say, "Here's a healthy, good-tasting diet." Bull. None of these diets taste as good as a good cheeseburger or a great steak or lobster. They just don't. So what we're doing is we're convincing ourselves that they do. It's all mental, because you convince yourself that it tastes as good. But it doesn't.

Do you want to know the best way to be healthy? Have parents with great genes. And if you made a bad choice, get new parents.

The number-one cause of death—is life.

It's just a thought. . . .

These days I'm often asked to participate in celebrity charity events. I once said yes to a downhill ski challenge that frankly I ought to have said no to. Betsy Bergman, head of affiliate relations for the show, tells the story like this:

Jerry and I were flying to Seattle for a charity ski challenge while we were on a West Coast affiliate visit. All of the planes out of Los Angles were delayed, so we missed the morning event, which Jerry was supposed to participate in. It was a race down a

bunny hill. Understand that Jerry hadn't been on skis in years, but he figured "what the heck . . . it's like riding a bike."

We finally made it to the mountain and the event coordinators threw these skis at Jerry and told him if he hurried he could make the next event. They put a microphone on him, and he headed to the chair lift. I've only skied twice in my life, and it was a zillion years ago, so thank God I didn't have to race.

So Jerry is riding up the lift with a reporter and they're chatting away; and as they get to the top of the mountain, Jerry turned around and realized he's doing a full downhill slalom course. The starter asked him if he wanted the red course or the blue. And poor Jerry, who's now white with panic, has no idea what this guy is talking about. But being a good sport comes easy for Jerry, so they put him in the box at the top of the run and the gate flies open. Now, Jerry couldn't exactly back out at this point, so he's flying down the mountain, not realizing he's supposed to go around the flags, forgetting he still has a microphone on, screaming obscenities all the way. He lived—but they didn't ask him back the next year.

A little footnote to that story. Betsy ended up trying to ski down after me, and she plowed into this group of skiers. I remember looking at her spread-eagled, face down on that mountain, her skis off, some woman's pole bent from the fall, one of the station executives wiped out.

I don't think we're on that station anymore.

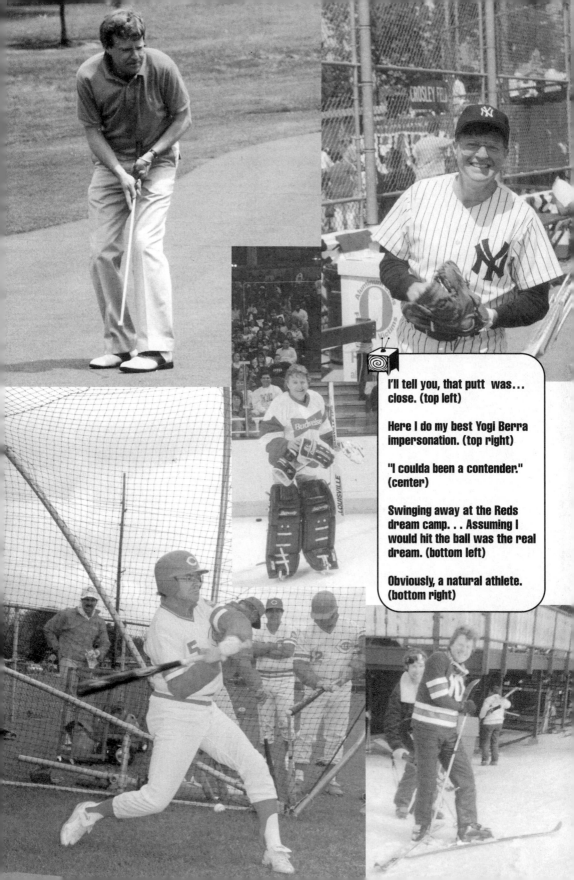

I'll tell you, that putt was... close. (top left)

Here I do my best Yogi Berra impersonation. (top right)

"I coulda been a contender." (center)

Swinging away at the Reds dream camp. . . Assuming I would hit the ball was the real dream. (bottom left)

Obviously, a natural athlete. (bottom right)

FOURTEEN
Favorite Final Thoughts

For those of you who watch my show, you know that I end each episode with what I call a "final thought." It is a summary of the topic, which I usually write the night before a show. Sometimes I end up changing my thoughts after we tape, but usually, based on my experience as host of the show—I stick with my original thought. I chose to include some of my favorite "final thoughts" in this book that appropriately tie into the stories I've shared. I hope you enjoy them. . . .

Final Thought: "I'm Making My First Adult Film"

For better or worse, in our culture we are defined by what we do. It is the second question we ask upon meeting someone: "Hi, what's your name?" Then, "What do you do?" A doctor, a teacher, a sales rep, a stripper. Each, fairly or not, paints an immediate picture of who this person is and, to a large extent, how he or she will be perceived, treated, respected . . . or perhaps not respected. So those who decide to pursue a career in the adult entertainment industry may, in fact, make some quick money. They may enjoy the momentary attention. The hours aren't bad, and it's not as if you need a lot of training or a particular skill.

But they only fool themselves if they ignore the reality——that this is no stepping stone to the future, either in terms of a career or in one's personal life.

It's not bad money for just stripping oneself of one's clothing. But when you strip yourself of your dignity, is any amount worth it?

Final Thought: "Drag Queen Waitresses"

It's a hellava show they put on . . . and that's all it is, a show, entertainment, fun. It's not sick, immoral, or the end of Western civilization as some self-annointed guardians of moral righteousness might suggest. No way. It shouldn't be taken that seriously.

I remember back when I was young, in the seemingly more conservative, innocent, and puritanical days of the fifties——the early days of television. Milton Berle was the biggest star. In fact, they called him Mr. Television . . . and his most popular weekly skit on his Tuesday night show was his dressing in drag. Nobody suggested perversion. It was pure entertainment. The classic movie of the age was *Some Like It Hot,* where, in pursuance of Marilyn Monroe, Jack Lemmon and Tony Curtis dressed in drag. Nobody was putting a damper on the moment with social commentary about the sinfulness of men dressing as women . . . and it's no different now with our guests today.

Their restaurant is a show . . . an evening out . . . to eat well and be entertained. And if we do nothing else but laugh or be amazed——and perhaps raise our level of tolerance for people and lifestyles that are simply different from ours——

then it's done well more than it's needed to. I understand that the food's pretty good, too. So if you like the service, don't be afraid to tip your waitress——even if she's really your waiter. It's not a sin.

Final Thought: "Exclusive: Adult Babies"

I'm always asked, as crazy as our show is, is there anything that's just too outrageous, I mean totally over the edge? And I can finally say "Yes." This is.

I confess, I don't pretend to understand this. Surely, this is America, and people are entitled to express themselves any way they wish, so long as they're not hurting anyone. But with all due respect, I understand how people can crave nurturing, and it's hard at times to escape the security of the crib, but this seems unsettling and totally repugnant to cultural norms. What's needed here is counseling . . . not diapers.

Final Thought: "Get Rid of That Jerk!"

We probably all know someone who's dating or married to someone we can't fathom. *What a jerk!* we think. *Surely she can do better than him. He mistreats her. He's no good. And what in God's name does she see in him?*

And yet, the more we offer our opinion, the more she seems to resist the advice and stick with him.

That's not to suggest the advice is bad——or that our opinion is necessarily wrong. It's just that if love isn't exactly blind, it at least passes over what it chooses not to see.

But if you simply harp on what a bum the boyfriend or husband is, she'll only start to resent you and become ever more defiant.

The best approach is to offer your advice only if asked, while constantly building up her own self-esteem by reminding her that no one ever has the right to mistreat her or disrespect her.

Perhaps then she'll reach a sensible conclusion about the man she's with on her own.

Love is great for us . . . but we don't always love who is great for us.

Final Thought: "I Cut Off My Manhood!"

This story stretches believability. Oh, I believe he cut off his organ. We checked that out. It's the reason he did it that defies belief. You're going to do that just to get a guy to lose interest? Become boring, don't return his calls, change your phone number, your cologne, yes, even your address. Yeah. If someone came up to me and said you can live in this neighborhood but lose your member, or live elsewhere and keep it, I'd be packing my bags before you could say U-Haul. Better to change your zip code than your reason for having a zipper. Clearly some professional counseling is needed here.

Simply put, if you're trying to cut off a relationship, make sure it's the relationship you're cutting.

Final Thought: "I Married a Horse!"

Surely this violates every biblical, moral, and legal dictate on the matter. I mean, if this isn't sick, what is? Our show, which is about outrageousness ... well, what is more outrageous than this?

And yet, there must be some psychological explanation——if not dysfunction——for this. We all love our pets, but heavy petting's about as far as it gets. To use an animal as a replacement for a human, to even be tempted toward such intimacy, suggests an immediate visit to the doctor.

You can love and admire the beauty and grace of a horse. You can pet it——and even bet on it. But if you're going to ride it, make sure you're up in the saddle.

Final Thought: "I'm Better Off Without You"

We often know what we want. We don't always know what's best for us. At least not initially. We are led by the heart, emotionally drawn and attached, and sometimes the relationship can be downright destructive. But we rationalize away the faults——blinded by this emotional dependency ——and we try and hang in however obvious it may seem to others that we ought to dump our mate.

The truth is, whenever the senses are involved, what is most pleasureable or intense isn't necessarily good.

Life is like a box of chocolates. No, you don't always know what you're going to get. But even if you did——and it's exactly what you want, and it tastes great——that doesn't

mean it's good for you. Sometimes you are better off without it——or him.

Final Thought: "I'm Pregnant by a Transsexual"

Like most people, I had difficulty understanding this issue.
I mean, I guess I always knew what gender I was. If I was
ever confused, a quick look in the mirror after stepping
out of the shower would remind me that, in fact, I was a
man. But I was never confused. I looked like a man, felt like
a man, and was attracted to women. It's never been an
issue——and that's true of most of us. But there are
those——of no less moral worth than the rest of us——who
from birth on just aren't that clear. Their genetic makeup
has left them confused when it comes to gender, and their
choices are simply to suppress it, deal with it, or, in the
extreme, medically change it.

If people are getting on Brittaney's case here today, it's
not because she's a transsexual, it's because the gender
confusion that permeates her life (which is not her fault) is
being visited upon others (which is her fault).

On a prior show, she admitted to deceiving men who
dated her, not telling them that she was a man.

Now she gets her lesbian lover pregnant, suggesting
additional unasked for problems for her baby-to-be——
growing up in a household where Dad's Mom, or is he?

The point is, now that Brittaney's about to be a parent,
it's time to put her own needs aside for the moment. The
child comes first. And while it's not necessary to put her

sexual preferences in the closet, it may not be a bad idea to put her dress there. The baby's entitled to some modicum of stability. There should be no confusion about that.

Final Thought: "Introduce Me to That Guest"

It's certainly not unusual for television stars, or even those less than stars, to be inundated by fan mail from viewers who like, or sometimes even love, what they see on their sets. And fed by their imaginations would simply do anything to actually meet this object of their affection. This soap star or prime-time character on their favorite sitcom.

And yet, if you think about it, this fan mail is directed at a person the viewer knows preciously little about. They know the role he or she plays on television and what gossip——most of which is made up——appears in the tabloids. But they don't know the real person. And yet the fan mail comes as if it's the love of a lifetime.

And so it shouldn't be too surprising that guests on talk shows receive fan mail as well, because at least here you get to see the real person——not an actor, not a fictitious character created for fantasy, but a real person with warts, flaws, and vulnerabilities exposed. That can be very appealing to someone looking for a friendship, a relationship, or more.

Maybe some of these encounters will turn into something, but warnings ought to be given. Yes, television is very powerful, but it can't replace real life. You can see a momentary snapshot of a person on the screen, but you can't possibly know the person through it. Indeed, what you see may not be what you get. Hopefully, what you find won't make you want to change the channel.

Final Thought: "Jerry's Christmas Show"

By tomorrow at this time the toys will have already been broken, the kids out of sorts from too much food and too little sleep, and we'll all have spent more than we said we would. But it all will have been worth it, for the post-holiday exhaustion is confirmation that we did it.

We upheld the tradition. We bludgeoned ourselves into irreversible fatigue. Indeed, we celebrated the family, and with everything else in the world and in our lives changing, that of all things, once again, did not. So the ritual survives, and in that predictability there is comfort and security.

Every time I hear somebody talk about Christmas, inevitably, they're talking about their childhood——the time Dad was out of work, so the stockings left for Santa were lean——but it was a great Christmas anyway because Mom made these dolls. Or the time Grandpa came home from the hospital in time for the holiday, but he wouldn't stay in bed, just so he could come down and play with the new set of electric trains under the tree.

It is always the memories, but not simply nostalgia. It is, instead, a concerted effort beginning shortly after Thanksgiving to recreate the holiday season we had as kids, just as our parents recreated their childhood for us. And our kids will recreate their joy for their children. We will work at it, often beyond what we can physically, emotionally, and financially afford, almost as if it's our one unchanging tie to past and future generations.

Our kids will grow up, move out, move away, and be different . . . but whatever they become, they will remember the moment when they were young, when they first saw the tree, when they didn't know quite how to say it, but they knew they were loved and they were never happier. And the fact that the ritual of overindulging is always too much, and always the same, and always a little bit silly, the point is, it is always.

And when you are talking about family, that's the nicest holiday gift of all——the fact that it is always . . . forever.

Final Thought: "Klanfrontation"

Admittedly these people are crazy, their racism unlikely to be taken seriously, hatemongers dressed up like clowns, but other than having children, they're hardly a threat to anyone.

And yet there is a point to be made here. Though they can be dismissed for being looney, their message, if ignored, can too easily become a growing cancer in our society. And it's not as if this hasn't happened before. Most of us like to think of such racism as barbaric——a behavior inconsistent with the values of a modern, educated Western culture. But it was a so-called highly civilized, cultured society in this century, in our lifetime, that visited the Holocaust on humanity. It was white, educated Europeans who came over here, slaughtered the Native Americans, brought blacks over as slaves, made discrimination against them legal till only a few years ago, and through the middle of this century.

Yes, some of the folks we saw today are nuts, and hardly worth losing any sleep over. But let's not leave today's show without thinking about how clean our record is on race, and prejudice and discrimination. Surely, most of us dress better, speak in politer tones, and appear far more cultured.

But remember, some of the most horrific things ever done to humans were done by the politest, best-dressed, most well-spoken people from the very best homes and neighborhoods.

If there's a lesson in all of this today, it's that we may all be offended by how they look——but what is really scary and dangerous are their ideas.

Final Thought: "Past Guests Face-Off"

"Where do you find these people?" It's the most asked question about talk shows——and yet, it's not as if the guests on these shows are a separate colony from the rest of society. Indeed, there are moments or facets in each of our lives that would make everybody else scratch their heads or take note or be amazed. The truth is, everybody has a talk show subject in them, and those who do choose to go on and bare their souls or dirty laundry or personal embarrassments are not suddenly forever separated from so-called "normal" society. In fact, what we saw today is that someone who strikes us as being outrageous or really different——or even shocking——is still capable of finding somebody else who is shocking or outrageous to them.

You see, we all seem to think we're normal, we're rational, we're stable and sensible. It's the other guy who's nuts. The lesson therefore being, that we better let everybody have their say 'cause for every time we want to silence someone 'cause we don't like their lifestyle, or what they believe or say, there's someone who thinks something of what *we* believe or what *we* are needs to be silenced as well.

Now please understand. No one's suggesting that all the values and ideas expressed by our guests today are of equal value. Not at all. Some are downright hurtful and morally void. But in a free society, of which we are so legitimately proud, that conclusion is reached, not because we silenced the other guy's argument, but rather because we heard it.

Final Thought: "The Holocaust Show"

Several years ago, before my parents died, I went to visit them in New York. My dad was seventy-eight at the time and he had this big old Chevrolet that he kept in the garage at the apartment building they lived in in Queens. He didn't drive it much anymore because frankly, it was too dangerous: his eyes weren't too good, his reflexes had slowed considerably and being really short, he could barely see over the steering wheel anyway. And my mom was deathly afraid every time he took it out for a ride. In fact, she refused to go along with him and begged him to please sell the car.

But he stubbornly refused, so Mom asked me, "Gerald, will you go talk to your dad and convince him to get rid of the car?"

Well, I really wasn't crazy about getting into the middle of it all, but Mom had a point. So I took Dad aside and said, "Pops, why don't you sell the car?"

"I'll tell you why," he told me. "You know, I don't drive it much anymore. In fact, I hardly drive it at all. I just want to know I have it here in case we've got to get away."

In case we've got to get away.

Understand, he was a bright man. He'd been living here in America for almost forty years. Nazi Germany and storm troopers and the concentration camps and the loss of our family, it was almost a lifetime ago——or so I thought. And how wrong I was. It suddenly hit me: the scars of a Holocaust are forever. Apparently, Dad never had a night where he didn't think it could all come back; he knew how fragile the character of civilization was.

But here's the good news. The same species that gave us the slime of a Hitler and his Nazi cohorts also can give us the bravest and most decent humans who graced our show today. I hope our kids were watching. I want them to know that there is good in this world, that there are heroes and not all of them hit home runs——some just open up their basements.

Final Thought: "Woman in Labor Confronts Mistress"

On most occasions, our show is primarily for entertainment. But even so, more often than not, there are lessons to be learned. We see how so often people mistreat each other in relationships; and if there's one common theme in these relationships from hell, it's that if the victim doesn't leave after the mistreatment, if she somehow believes that she can change him, that he'll be sorry for what he did, he won't do it again, he'll be good from now on, well, the fact is, she's bound to be disappointed. You can take it to the bank; she's going to be stepped on again. We've said it so often it's become a virtual certainty. People get treated the way they permit themselves to be treated. And so long as she stays and puts up with his infidelity and kids herself into believing that she'll change him, he'll continue to behave badly, simply because he can and she lets him.

The best way to get treated with respect is to demand it——and accept nothing less.

Final Thought: "Zack the Seventy-Pound Baby"

To be honest, we were part of the stampede, the media rush to get this lovable large toddler on the air, to share his story and that of his family with the world. We, like most other people, are fascinated with anything or anyone who is out of the ordinary . . . and Zack is.

And yet this is not a freak show. This is Mom and Dad desperately seeking help for a condition they cannot explain and, at least to this point, seem unable to alleviate.

For each of us who has ever had a child of our own, we know the extra prayers, the crossed fingers, the held breath that everything will be okay, that all the parts will be as they should be in working order, that our child will be, above all, healthy and happy.

Having received no satisfaction thus far, who among us wouldn't do anything we could——including running to the media——to get help? Obviously, television and news-papers can't help everyone. There are heart-wrenching stories that never make it to the front page or on anyone's show, but the stories that do get covered should serve as a reminder that a perfectly healthy, normal child is a miracle for which we must be eternally thankful. And the way we say thanks is to offer compassion, caring, and, where pos-sible, help to those children who, perhaps, face a few bumps in the road of life.

The "Zacks" of the world must know that the world isn't just staring at them——but caring about them.

'TIL NEXT TIME, TAKE CARE OF YOURSELF . . . AND EACH OTHER.

FIFTEEN
Jerry Springer Show Titles

1991–1992 SEASON

AIR DATE   TITLE

AIR DATE	TITLE
09/30/91	"Reunion Show"
10/01/91	"Ethnic Dating Game"
10/02/91	"Children Face Death"
10/03/91	"Crisis Makeovers"
10/04/91	"Phone Moms"
10/07/91	"AIDS as a Weapon"
10/08/91	"My Child Grew Up in a Hospital"
10/09/91	"My Kids Won't Stop Fighting"
10/10/91	"Single People: On the Outside Looking In"
10/11/91	"My Parents' Divorce Ruined My Life"
10/14/91	"When Jerry Met Sally (Jessy)"
10/15/91	"Raped, Tortured and Still Alive"
10/16/91	"Four Is Enough"
10/17/91	"My Kid Won't Stop Eating"
10/18/91	"Who's a Better Mom?"
10/21/91	"I Gave Myself an Abortion"
10/22/91	"Sexual Harassment"
10/23/91	"Is There a God?"
10/24/91	"Incest"
10/25/91	"Do Fat People Make Better Lovers?"

10/28/91	"My Fiancé Won't Marry Me Until I Stop Stripping"
10/29/91	"Jerry Joins the Homeless"
10/30/91	"I Check the Mail 50 Times a Day"
10/31/91	"I Hate Going Outside to Smoke"
11/01/91	"They Stole My Husband's Eyes"
11/04/91	"Defending Your Family Without a Gun"
11/05/91	"I Woke Up in the Morgue"
11/06/91	"I Hit Rock Bottom, Now I'm on Top"
11/07/91	"Sneaking Around with a Black Man"
11/08/91	"I'm 16 and My Life Is Ruined"
11/11/91	"Mommy, Why Won't You Pay My Child Support?"
11/12/91	"I Love My Mother So Much, I'll Kill Her"
11/13/91	"Protesting with Porn"
11/14/91	"Is Hypnotism Real?"
11/15/91	"I Turned My Head, and My Child Is Dead"
11/18/91	"Charity Frauds"
11/19/91	"Addicted to Love"
11/20/91	"Young Killers"
11/21/91	"The Lottery Will Send You to Hell"
11/25/91	"Makeover Madness"
11/26/91	"Breaking the Rules"
11/27/91	"Why Can't I Raise a Different Race Child?"
12/02/91	"Pornography Destroyed My Life"
12/03/91	"That's No Woman, She's a He!"
12/04/91	"My Spending Was Out of Control"
12/05/91	"Spoiled Brats or Rotten Parents?"
12/06/91	"The Lord Has Ruined My Life"
12/09/91	"Men That Women Hate"
12/10/91	"Abstinence vs. Safe Sex"
12/11/91	"The Newlywed Game"
12/12/91	"I Left My Wife for Another Man"
12/13/91	"A Ghost Threw Me Down the Stairs"
12/16/91	"Do Killers Deserve to Go Free?"
12/17/91	"We Met in the Personals"
12/18/91	"Topless Dancers and Their Sins"

12/19/91	"I Worshiped Satan at Age 6"
12/20/91	"Child Alcoholics"
01/06/92	"Men Who Like Their Women Mean"
01/07/92	"Update Show"
01/08/92	"Women Without Hair"
01/09/92	"Adoption Reunions Gone Bad"
01/10/92	"I Want to Be Sexier"
01/13/92	"Your Words Are Killing Me"
01/14/92	"Multiple Personality Disorder"
01/15/92	"I Have a Disease and the Doctors Won't Treat Me"
01/16/92	"Older Women & Younger Men"
01/17/92	"I Married a PMS Monster"
01/20/92	"Aliens"
01/21/92	"Pregnant Women Need Not Apply"
01/22/92	"My Doctor Never Went to Med School"
01/23/92	"Gun Control"
01/24/92	"Stage Mothers and Their Little Stars"
01/27/92	"My Brother Killed 24 Children"
01/28/92	"I Hate the Way My Sister Dresses"
01/29/92	"I'm Suing My Dad for Rape"
01/30/92	"Oliver North: an American Hero"
01/31/92	"Springer's Court"
02/03/92	"Lingerie Fantasies"
02/04/92	"I Sold My Baby"
02/05/92	"I Can't Get over Elvis"
02/06/92	"Phone Sex Killed My Husband"
02/07/92	"My Therapist, My Lover"
02/10/92	"Springer's Dating Conection"
02/11/92	"I'm Fat & I'm Proud"
02/12/92	"I Do Drugs at Church"
02/13/92	"Do-It-Yourself Abortions"
02/14/92	"Homosexual Cures"
02/17/92	"My Dad Wears Women's Clothing"
02/18/92	"The Sexual Beast in You"
02/19/92	"Buy American"

02/20/92	"Blue Collar Hunks Pageant"
02/21/92	"Jealous Men & Their Wives"
02/24/92	"Circus Freaks"
02/25/92	"Fantasy Makeovers"
02/26/92	"Girls in the Gang"
02/27/92	"Nude Maids & Hot Dog Babes"
02/28/92	"Death over Designer Clothes"
03/02/92	"Help! I'm Being Stalked"
03/03/92	"Men Who Love Boys"
03/04/92	"I Hate Being Blonde"
03/05/92	"Mother's Controlling My Life"
03/06/92	"Home Nudity"
03/09/92	"Adult Fun & Games"
03/10/92	"Ladies Who Steal"
03/11/92	"I'm Old & I Love It"
03/12/92	"Families That Fight"
03/16/92	"Outrageous Psychics"
03/17/92	"I Hate My Son's Long Hair"
03/18/92	"I'm Fighting for My Grandchildren"
03/19/92	"Gossip Almost Made Me Kill Myself"
03/23/92	"Dwarves Are People Too"
03/24/92	"Moms Addicted to Gambling"
03/25/92	"The Police Murdered My Son"
03/26/92	"Faith Healers"
03/30/92	"My Husband's a Fat Slob"
03/31/92	"I Didn't Know I Married a Rapist"
04/01/92	"Addicted to Dieting"
04/02/92	"I Saved My Twin's Life"
04/06/92	"Ali MacGraw"
04/07/92	"My Son Is a Rapist"
04/08/92	"Suicide Blackmail"
04/09/92	"Innocent People Who Went to Jail"
04/13/92	"Meddling Mothers-in-Law"
04/14/92	"Children Without a Conscience"

04/15/92	"I Hate Being Beautiful"
04/16/92	"Indians and Racism"
04/17/92	"Battered Men"
04/20/92	"I Spied on My Spouse"
04/21/92	"I Despise Interracial Couples"
04/22/92	"Girls Dancing for Girls"
04/23/92	"Street Kids"
04/24/92	"My Mother Flirts with Me"
04/27/92	"Big-Breasted Women"
04/28/92	"I'm Fighting to Be a Transsexual"
04/29/92	"Making Love Behind Bars"
04/30/92	"Street Kid Follow-up"
05/01/92	"Dead Babies on TV"
05/04/92	"Playgirl Centerfold Dream Dates"
05/05/92	"Richard Simmons"
05/06/92	"Teen Vampires"
05/07/92	"Rodney King Verdict"
05/08/92	"Homosexual Boy Scouts"
05/11/92	"Life in the Ghetto"
05/12/92	"Male Stripper Competition"
05/13/92	"Cheapskates"
05/14/92	"Angry Teens"
05/15/92	"I Was Duped by a Sailor"
05/18/92	"I Want My Daughter's School Books Banned"
05/19/92	"I Was Born a Boy and a Girl"
05/20/92	"Women Who Think Black Men Are No Good"
05/21/92	"Women Who Think Black Men Are No Good, Pt. 2"
05/22/92	"Who Is Jesse Jackson?"
05/25/92	"Private Lives of Ministers' Wives"
05/26/92	"I Was Tortured by My Mother"
05/27/92	"I Want My Wife to Look Sexy"
05/28/92	"My 10-Year-Old Daughter Was Raped by 5 Boys"
05/29/92	"Men Who Think They Know What Women Want"
06/01/92	"Help Me Stop Spoiling My Kids"
06/02/92	"I Want AIDS/HIV Patients Quarantined"

06/03/92	"911 Caused My Son's Death"
06/04/92	"I Can't Get over My High School Sweetheart"
06/05/92	"Bizarre Diseases"
06/08/92	"A Lesbian Marriage"
06/09/92	"I Live with a Nag"
06/10/92	"My Classmates Beat Me Up"
06/11/92	"I Can't Stop Lying"
06/12/92	"Porno Saved My Marriage"
06/15/92	"Beer, Broads, & TV: Real Life Al Bundys"
06/16/92	"Obnoxious Little League Parents"
06/17/92	"I Gave Birth to an Albino"
06/18/92	"Modern Day Robin Hoods"
06/19/92	"From Nerd to Knockout"
06/22/92	"I Buy It, Wear It, & Take It Back"
06/23/92	"I'm Part of a Ménage à Trois"
06/24/92	"I Only Have a Dad"
06/25/92	"Police Psychic Finds Missing Children"
06/26/92	"My Parrot Runs My Life"
06/30/92	"We Lived a Wedding Day Nightmare"
07/01/92	"How to Spice Up Your Sex Life"
07/02/92	"Wheelchair Wonders"
07/03/92	"My Son Was Stabbed by His 6-Year-Old Schoolmate"
07/06/92	"What I Did for Revenge"
07/07/92	"I'm Mentally Disabled and I'm Married"
07/08/92	"I Might Die of a Broken Heart"
07/09/92	"I've Never Seen My Sister"
07/10/92	"I Watched My Mother Murder My Brothers & Sister"

1996–1997 SEASON

09/02/96	"Help Me Find My Family"
09/03/96	"1000 Shows"
09/04/96	"Real-Life 'X-Files' "
09/05/96	"We Live in a Car"
09/06/96	"We Still Live in a Car"
09/09/96	"I Have 15 Personalities"
09/10/96	"I Have Six Wives"
09/11/96	"I Do. . . . I Don't"
09/12/96	"Love Against the Odds"
09/13/96	"This Relationship's Over"
09/16/96	"Zack . . . The 70-Pound Baby"
09/17/96	"Why Did You Do It?"
09/18/96	"Please Leave Us Alone"
09/19/96	"Get Rid of That Man"
09/20/96	"Unusual Candidates"
09/23/96	"My Wife Weighs 900 Pounds"
09/24/96	"Torn Between Two Women"
09/25/96	"My Marriage Is a Mistake"
09/26/96	"Stop What You're Doing . . . Now!"
09/27/96	"Back Off . . . He's Mine"
09/30/96	"Past Guests Face-Off"
10/01/96	"Why Are You Together?"
10/02/96	"You're Ex Is Breaking Us Up"
10/03/96	"I'm Better Off Without You"
10/04/96	"Street Performers"
10/07/96	"I'm Sorry, I Cheated"
10/08/96	"I'm Jealous of My Gay Friend"
10/09/96	"That Man Will Ruin You!"
10/10/96	"Divorce Him!"
10/11/96	"I Was Born Both Male and Female"
10/14/96	"Jerry Updates Past Couples"
10/15/96	"Stay Away from My Daughters"

10/16/96	"The Execution of Frankie Parker"
10/17/96	"I Want My Wife Back!"
10/18/96	"Springer Staff's Favorite Shows"
10/21/96	"Battling Sisters"
10/22/96	"I Can't Stop Dating Convicts"
10/23/96	"Get Away from Him"
10/25/96	"Bernard Goetz: Subway Gunman"
10/28/96	"I Hate Who You're With"
10/29/96	"Reunions!"
10/30/96	"I Hate My Son's Wife"
10/31/96	"Female Chain Gang"
11/01/96	"Did They Lose the Weight?"
11/04/96	"Jerry Rescues an Obese Man"
11/05/96	"Update: Get Rid of That Man"
11/06/96	"KKK Moms"
11/07/96	"I'm Proud to Be a Prostitute"
11/08/96	"My 15-Year-Old Son Wears a Dress"
11/11/96	"Zack's Back!"
11/12/96	"I'm in Love with a Serial Killer"
11/13/96	"I Hate Your Sexy Job"
11/14/96	"Update: Love Against the Odds"
11/15/96	"The Mole People"
11/18/96	"Men Who Work as Women"
11/19/96	"High-Class Call Girls"
11/20/96	"My Brother Stole My Wife"
11/21/96	"Klan Families"
11/22/96	"I'm on the Verge of Divorce"
11/25/96	"I Want Your Man"
11/26/96	"My Man's Behaving Badly"
11/27/96	"The Man with 8 Wives"
11/28/96	"I Won't Date My Race"
11/29/96	"I'm a Teenage Junkie"
12/16/96	"My Man's a Cheater"
12/17/96	"I'm a Homeless Teen"

12/18/96	"I'll Do Anything to Get You Back"
12/19/96	"A Psychic Contacts the Dead"
12/23/96	"We're in Holiday Hell!"
12/24/96	"Dear Santa . . . "
12/25/96	"Happy Holidays"
12/26/96	"Reunions for the Holiday"
12/27/96	"Do You Want Me or Not?"
01/13/97	"Jerry, Help Me Meet That Guest"
01/14/97	"I've Fallen for My Best Friend"
01/15/97	"My Man Needs to Shape Up"
01/16/97	"It's Now . . . or Never!"
01/17/97	"Exotic Dancers"
01/20/97	"I Want Only You"
01/21/97	"Sexy Makeovers"
01/22/97	"Do You Want Me . . . or Her?"
01/23/97	"I Still Love My Ex"
01/24/97	"Jerry vs. Larry Flynt"
01/27/97	"Rodney Dangerfield"
01/28/97	"You'll Never Be in My Family"
01/29/97	"You Stole My Man"
01/30/97	"Secret Fantasies"
01/31/97	"Shock Rock"
02/03/97	"I Want Out of This Threesome"
02/04/97	"I'm Still in 8th Grade and I'm Pregnant"
02/05/97	"My Wife Wants to Be a Call Girl"
02/06/97	"Tijuana Strip Club Girls"
02/07/97	"Lori & Dori"
02/10/97	"Behind the Scenes of an Adult Film"
02/11/97	"Are You Cheating?"
02/12/97	"Why I Sell My Body"
02/13/97	"Teenage Drag Queens"
02/14/97	"A Night with the Miami PD"
02/17/97	"I'm Making My First Adult Film"
02/18/97	"Update: My Family Stole My Baby"

02/19/97	"It's Your Baby . . . and I Have Proof"
02/20/97	"I'm 12 and I Take Care of My 680-Pound Mom"
02/21/97	"Close That Strip Club Down!"
02/24/97	"My Girlfriend's a Guy"
02/25/97	"A Woman Confronts Her Sexual Attacker"
02/26/97	"That Man's No Good"
02/27/97	"Teen Girls Gone Wild"
02/28/97	"No Blacks Allowed (in My Neighborhood)"
03/10/97	"I'm Having Your Husband's Baby"
03/11/97	"I Had a Sex Change at 50 Years Old"
03/12/97	"Our Daughter Was Murdered"
03/13/97	"Surprise . . . I Slept with Your Man"
03/14/97	"Unusual Love Triangles"
03/17/97	"Dr. Dre and Ed Lover's Favorite Shows"
03/18/97	"Update: Bad Relationships"
03/19/97	"Black Supremacists vs. White Supremacists"
03/20/97	"Hollywood Boulevard Girls"
03/21/97	"Relationships on the Rocks"
03/24/97	"Your Lifestyle Will Ruin Us"
03/25/97	"We Just Fulfilled Our Fantasy"
03/26/97	"Prostitute Moms"
03/28/97	"My Fiancé Wants Me to Be a Racist"
03/31/97	"Update: That Serial Killer Was My Father"
04/01/97	"Our Love Life Is in Trouble"
04/02/97	"My 6th-Grade Daughter's in a Gang"
04/03/97	"Update: Unforgettable Guests (Lori & Dori)"
04/04/97	"Since the Last Show"
04/07/97	"My Sister Is Pregnant by My Ex"
04/08/97	"I'm 16 and My Husband Is 36!"
04/09/97	"I'm Here to Break You Up"
04/10/97	"Jerry Helps Reunite Families"
04/11/97	"Get Away from My Man!"
04/21/97	"Male Siamese Twins"
04/22/97	"Pregnant and Dumped"
04/23/97	"Stop Stalking My Man"

04/24/97	"I'm a Breeder for the Klan"
04/25/97	"My Brother's a Pimp"
04/28/97	"My Boyfriend Is a Girl"
04/29/97	"Before We Marry . . . I Must Confess"
04/30/97	"Give Up Your Sexy Job"
05/01/97	"Past Guests Confront"
05/02/97	"I'm a Teen Call Girl"
05/05/97	"Wild Ways to Make a Living"
05/06/97	"Surprise . . . I Have a Secret Lover"
05/07/97	"I Want to Be a Centerfold"
05/08/97	"My Sister Stole My Husband"
05/12/97	"I'm 7-Months Pregnant and Still Stripping"
05/13/97	"I've Got to Tell You . . . "
05/14/97	"On-line Strippers and Escorts"
05/15/97	"We Had a One-Night Stand"
05/16/97	"Jenna Jamison: Sex Goddess"
05/19/97	"Update: My Boyfriend Is Really a Girl"
05/20/97	"My Mother's Girlfriend Is 17"
05/21/97	"Update: 12-Year-Old Girl and Her 680-Pound Mom"
05/22/97	"I Have Something to Tell You"
05/23/97	"Stop Selling Your Body"
06/16/97	"I Hate My Girlfriend's Sexy Job"
06/17/97	"I Know You're Cheating!"
06/18/97	"My Girlfriend Is Really a Man!"
06/19/97	"My Son Weighs 500 Pounds!"
06/20/97	"Dumped on Springer"
06/23/97	"I Want to Strip for My Man"
06/24/97	"You're Better Off Single!"
06/25/97	"You'll Never Marry Our Daughter"
06/26/97	"Update: Exotic Dancers"
06/27/97	"Update: Our Brother Is a Pimp"
06/30/97	"I Stole My Sister's Husband"
07/01/97	"I'm Marrying a Transsexual"
07/02/97	"I'm Here to Dump You"
07/03/97	"My Relationship Is on the Rocks"

07/04/97	"I Can't Forgive My Man"
07/07/97	"Comics on Delivery"
07/08/97	"Be Honest . . . Are You Cheating?"
07/09/97	"Choose Me or Lose Me"
07/10/97	"I'm Sleeping with Your Man"
07/11/97	"Surprise . . . Meet My New Lover"
07/14/97	"I Cut Off My Manhood!"
07/15/97	"Update: My Sister Stole My Husband"
07/17/97	"Paternity Tests Revealed"
07/18/97	"I Broke the World's Sex Record"
07/21/97	"I Want to Be a Teen Stripper"
07/22/97	"I Have a Secret to Tell You"
07/23/97	"I'm Really a Man"
07/24/97	"KKK Parents"
07/25/97	"It's Your Bachelor Party or Me"
07/28/97	"I Make a Sexy Living"
07/29/97	"I Stole My 12-Year-Old's Boyfriend"
07/30/97	"I Have Many Lovers"
07/31/97	"Past Couples Confronted"
08/01/97	"Adult Film Stars Tell All"
08/04/97	"I've Been Keeping a Secret"
08/05/97	"I Can't Let You Get Married"
08/06/97	"Teens Out of Control"
08/07/97	"Big-Busted Strippers (Daytona)"
08/08/97	"I Want to Be a Sex Star (Daytona)"
08/11/97	"I Want to Join a Suicide Cult"
08/12/97	"You're Too Fat to Dress Like That"
08/13/97	"Update: Female Chain Gang"
08/14/97	"Get Out of Our Relationship"
08/15/97	"Sideshow Freaks"
08/18/97	"I'm Proud to Be a Racist"
08/19/97	"My Sister Ruined My Life"
08/20/97	"It's Over—Get over It"
08/22/97	"I Want a Sexy Job"

1997–1998 SEASON

09/22/97	"I Have a Secret. . . . I'm a Call Girl!"
09/23/97	"Stay Away from My Lover!"
09/24/97	"My Teen Worships Satan"
09/25/97	"I'm a First-Time Stripper"
09/26/97	"Surprise! I Have a Bisexual Lover"
09/29/97	"You Stole My Lover"
09/30/97	"I'm Cheating on You"
10/01/97	"I'm Pregnant by My Kidnapper"
10/02/97	"I'm Here to Steal Your Lover"
10/03/97	"The Klan Files"
10/06/97	"You're a Homewrecker!"
10/07/97	"Update: I Cut Off My Manhood!"
10/08/97	"My Girlfriend Is a Cheater!"
10/09/97	"A Teenager's Pregnant with My Man's Baby"
10/10/97	"Leave My Man Alone!"
10/13/97	"Wife Discovers Husband's Secret Family"
10/14/97	"I've Been Unfaithful!"
10/15/97	"Quit the Klan!"
10/16/97	"I'm Pregnant . . . Stop Cheating!"
10/17/97	"Past Guests Get Revenge!"
10/20/97	"You Have One More Chance!"
10/21/97	"I'm in a Love Triangle!"
10/22/97	"Klanfrontation"
10/23/97	"I Love You . . . Both!"
10/24/97	"Paternity Results: I Slept with Two Brothers!"
10/27/97	"I Hate Your Sexy Occupation"
10/28/97	"Get Rid of Your Lover!"
10/29/97	"Tell Her It's Over"
10/30/97	"Woman in Labor Confronts Mistress"
10/31/97	"My Pimp Won't Let Me Go!"
11/03/97	"I'm Pregnant by a Transsexual"
11/04/97	"You'll Never Marry My Brother!"

11/05/97	"I'm Pregnant by Your Man!"
11/06/97	"Why'd You Cheat?"
11/07/97	"Honey, I'm Really a Guy"
11/10/97	"Bachelorette Party Fights!"
11/11/97	"Past Guests Do Battle!"
11/12/97	"Pregnant Bad Girls"
11/13/97	"Give Up, It's Over!"
11/14/97	"I Have a Secret Lover!"
11/17/97	"You Dumped Me at the Altar!"
11/18/97	"It's Either Me or Her!"
11/19/97	"Guess What . . . I'm Bisexual!"
11/20/97	"Hands Off My Lover!"
11/21/97	"I Refuse to Wear Clothes"
11/24/97	"I Will Break You Up"
11/25/97	"Surprise! I Have Two Lovers!"
11/26/97	"I'm 16 and in a Love Triangle"
12/01/97	"1,200th Show Party!"
12/02/97	"Who's the Father of My Baby?"
12/03/97	"I'm a 14-Year-Old Prostitute"
12/04/97	"Dumped While Pregnant"
12/05/97	"My Niece Stole My Husband"
12/08/97	"I'm Pregnant & I Have to Strip"
12/09/97	"I Can't Stay Faithful"
12/10/97	"Before We Marry . . . I Have a Secret"
12/11/97	"You Can't Have Us Both"
12/12/97	"I Love Two Women!"
12/15/97	"Update: Woman in Labor Confronts Mistress"
12/16/97	"I'm Here to Stop Your Wedding!"
12/17/97	"Leave That Loser!"
12/18/97	"It's Not Over . . . Yet!"
12/19/97	"You Won't Ruin My Relationship!"
01/01/98	"Teen Girls with Older Men"
01/12/98	"I'm Having a Secret Affair!"
01/13/98	"Stop Sleeping with My Lover!"

01/14/98	"Jerry Rescues a 1,200-Pound Couple"
01/15/98	"Teenage Call Girls"
01/16/98	"Give Back My Lover!"
01/19/98	"I Won't Let You Get Married!"
01/20/98	"A Teenager's Pregnant with My Man's Baby"
01/21/98	"Bachelorette Party Fights"
01/22/98	"You Have One More Chance!"
01/23/98	"I Have a Secret to Tell You"
01/26/98	"Dump Your Lover . . . You're Mine!"
01/27/98	"It's Your Mother or Me!"
01/28/98	"I'm Married but Live with My Lover"
01/29/98	"I'll Destroy Your Relationship"
01/30/98	"I've Been Keeping a Secret"
02/02/98	"Stripper Wars!"
02/03/98	"You Can't Have My Man!"
02/04/98	"You're Destroying My Family!"
02/05/98	"I Have a Surprise . . . I'm Cheating"
02/06/98	"I Have Too Many Lovers!"
02/09/98	"Holiday Hell Feast!"
02/10/98	"I Want Your Lover!"
02/11/98	"I Have a Bizarre Sex Life"
02/12/98	"Update: I Still Love You"
02/13/98	"I Have a Secret for My Man!"
02/16/98	"I'll Never Let You Go"
02/17/98	"I Have Sex with My Sister"
02/18/98	"Past Guests Attack!"
02/19/98	"Home Wreckers Confronted!"
02/20/98	"Honey . . . I'm a Call Girl"
02/23/98	"I'll Fight for My Man"
02/24/98	"I'm Having a Bisexual Affair"
02/25/98	"My Lover Is a Cheat!"
02/26/98	"I Won't Let You Sell Your Body!"
02/27/98	"Guess What . . . I'm a Man!"
03/02/98	"I've Had Enough . . . It's Over!"
03/03/98	"I Have a Sexy Secret"

RINGMASTER!

03/04/98	"Get Your Own Man!"
03/23/98	"Prostitutes vs. Pimps"
03/24/98	"Your Man Wants Me!"
03/25/98	"I Slept with Your Lover!"
03/26/98	"I'm Here to Divorce You!"
03/27/98	"Adult Babies"
03/30/98	"Attack of the Ex-Lovers"
03/31/98	"Viewers Battle the Klan"
04/01/98	"I Have Another Lover"
04/02/98	"Updates: Teens with Older Lovers"
04/03/98	"I Have a Wild Sex Job"
04/06/98	"Newlyweds Headed for Divorce"
04/07/98	"Dump Your Cheating Lover!"
04/08/98	"I Share My Lover!"
04/09/98	"Why Did We Marry? You're Gay!"
04/10/98	"You Can't Have Him"
04/13/98	"I'm Here to Confront My One-Night Stand!"
04/14/98	"He Doesn't Want You! He's Mine!"
04/15/98	"It's Time to Choose!"
04/16/98	"Out-of-Control Teens"
04/17/98	"Lovers vs. Mistresses"
04/20/98	"Dumped for Another Lover"
04/21/98	"Torn Between Two Lovers"
04/22/98	"My Daugther Is a Teen Prostitute"
04/23/98	"I'm Pregnant by My Brother"
04/24/98	"Bizarre Love Triangles"
04/27/98	"Wives Battle Mistresses"
04/28/98	"I'm Hiding a Sexy Secret"
04/29/98	"Update: You'll Never Marry My Brother"
04/30/98	"Ex-Lovers Confronted"
04/31/98	"Surprise, I'm a Transsexual"
05/04/98	"Surprise, I Have a Secret Sex Life"
05/05/98	"Mistresses Attack!"
05/06/98	"I Have a Secret!"
05/07/98	"My Pimp Runs My Family"

05/08/98	"I Have a Wild Lifestyle"
05/11/98	"I'm Cheating on My Lover!"
05/12/98	"My Uncle Stole My Wife"
05/13/98	"Hidden Truths Revealed"
05/14/98	"Like It or Not, I'm Pregnant"
05/15/98	"Quit Your Sexy Job . . . Or Else!"
05/18/98	"600-Pound Angry Mom"
05/19/98	"Stripper Love Triangles"
05/20/98	"Invasion of the Past Guests"
05/21/98	"Butt Out of Our Threesome"
05/22/98	"I Married a Horse" (has this show date but did not air)
06/15/98	"I Must Confess . . . I'm a Cheater"
06/16/98	"Update: I'm a Wild Teen"
06/17/98	*"Springer's* Travels"
06/18/98	"Wild & Sexy Affairs"
06/19/98	"My Granny Robbed the Cradle!"
06/22/98	"I'll Do Anything to Break You Up!"
06/23/98	"Pregnant to Trap"
06/24/98	"I'm Sleeping with Your Lover"
06/25/98	"Update: Most Fascinating People"
06/26/98	"Bizarre Sex Jobs"
06/29/98	"My Ex Won't Leave Me Alone!"
06/30/98	"It's Over . . . but I Still Want You!"
07/01/98	"I'll Make My Choice Today"
07/02/98	"Family Affairs"
07/03/98	"I'm Not the Home Wrecker . . . You Are!"
07/06/9	"War of the Past Guests"
07/07/98	"Love, Springer Style!"
07/08/98	"Stop Sleeping with My Man!"
07/09/98	"Mom, Will You Marry Me?"
07/10/98	"Secret Bisexual Affairs"
07/13/98	"Lovers Battle Mistresses"
07/14/98	"Battle of the Babes"
07/15/98	"I'm Sleeping with My Sister's Fiancé!"

RINGMASTER!

07/16/98	"Your Lover Wants Me!"
07/17/98	"Lesbian Love Affairs"
07/20/98	"My Sister and I Have Sex"
07/21/98	"I Had a Baby with Your Man!"
07/22/98	"Marriage Confessions"
07/23/98	"I Want Another Lover!"
07/24/98	"Update: Transsexual Secrets"
07/27/98	"I Have Sex with My Twin"
07/28/98	"I Can't Stop Cheating!"
07/29/98	"Conflicting Lovers Return"
07/30/98	"You Won't Steal My Lover!"
07/31/98	"Dumped for a One-Night Stand"
08/03/98	"I'm Sleeping with My 13-Year-Old's Ex"
08/04/98	"I Hate Your Lover!"
08/05/98	"Update: Outrageous Guests"
08/06/98	"Green Room Secrets"
08/07/98	"Love Triangle Ultimatums"

It's a Crazy World . . . Have Fun with It . . .

Photo Credits

191 Todd Buchanan	(Double hair pull)
194 Todd Buchanan	(Cat fight)
197 Todd Buchanan	(Man attacking transsexual lover)
198 Todd Buchanan	(Girl slapping man)
205 Scott Barbour	(Jerry selling Too Hot)
217 John P. Johnson	(Jerry in cowboy outfit on movie)
219 Rafael Winer	(Girl sitting on Jerry's desk in movie)
220 Jerry Springer	(Micki)
223 Mimi Fuller	(Jerry and Micki with Katie on steps)
225 Jerry Springer	(Katie)
228 Jerry Springer	(Playing baseball at camp)
232 Kathy Posner & Comm 2	(Jerry as Mr. America)
235 Jerry Springer	(Jerry in Yankee outfit)
235 Wally Brinbach	(Jerry putting)
235 Tom Robinson	(Jerry in Reds outfit)
235 Laurie Fried	(Jerry as hockey goalie)
235 Harry Goldsmith	(Jerry skiing)